CAMBRIDGE LIBRARY COLLECTION

Books of enduring scholarly value

History

The books reissued in this series include accounts of historical events and movements by eye-witnesses and contemporaries, as well as landmark studies that assembled significant source materials or developed new historiographical methods. The series includes work in social, political and military history on a wide range of periods and regions, giving modern scholars ready access to influential publications of the past.

Imperial Defence

The liberal Radical MP Sir Charles Wentworth Dilke (1843–1911) campaigned for (among many other causes) votes for women and labourers, legalisation of trade unions, and universal education. His republican sentiments damaged his political reputation, and earned him the hostility of Queen Victoria. However, despite his views on the monarchy he was an imperialist, and his early work, *Greater Britain* (1868; also available in this series), was widely read. In the 1890s he became known as a parliamentary expert on military, colonial and foreign affairs. This 1892 work, co-written with Spenser Wilkinson (1853–1937), a journalist and military historian, together with Dilke's earlier work, *Problems of Greater Britain*, led to the founding of a parliamentary committee on imperial defence. The book argues that, while hoping to avert war by diplomacy, the Government has a duty to maintain a naval and military force to protect the interests of its citizens.

Cambridge University Press has long been a pioneer in the reissuing of out-of-print titles from its own backlist, producing digital reprints of books that are still sought after by scholars and students but could not be reprinted economically using traditional technology. The Cambridge Library Collection extends this activity to a wider range of books which are still of importance to researchers and professionals, either for the source material they contain, or as landmarks in the history of their academic discipline.

Drawing from the world-renowned collections in the Cambridge University Library and other partner libraries, and guided by the advice of experts in each subject area, Cambridge University Press is using state-of-the-art scanning machines in its own Printing House to capture the content of each book selected for inclusion. The files are processed to give a consistently clear, crisp image, and the books finished to the high quality standard for which the Press is recognised around the world. The latest print-on-demand technology ensures that the books will remain available indefinitely, and that orders for single or multiple copies can quickly be supplied.

The Cambridge Library Collection brings back to life books of enduring scholarly value (including out-of-copyright works originally issued by other publishers) across a wide range of disciplines in the humanities and social sciences and in science and technology.

Imperial Defence

CHARLES WENTWORTH DILKE
SPENSER WILKINSON

CAMBRIDGE UNIVERSITY PRESS

Cambridge, New York, Melbourne, Madrid, Cape Town,
Singapore, São Paolo, Delhi, Mexico City

Published in the United States of America by Cambridge University Press, New York

www.cambridge.org
Information on this title: www.cambridge.org/9781108044738

© in this compilation Cambridge University Press 2012

This edition first published 1892
This digitally printed version 2012

ISBN 978-1-108-04473-8 Paperback

IMPERIAL DEFENCE

IMPERIAL DEFENCE

BY THE RIGHT HONOURABLE

Sir CHARLES WENTWORTH DILKE, Bart.

AUTHOR OF "GREATER BRITAIN," AND "PROBLEMS OF GREATER BRITAIN"

AND

SPENSER WILKINSON

AUTHOR OF "CITIZEN SOLDIERS," AND "THE BRAIN OF AN ARMY"

LONDON

MACMILLAN AND CO.

AND NEW YORK

1892

LONDON:

PRINTED BY WILLIAM CLOWES AND SONS, LIMITED,

STAMFORD STREET AND CHARING CROSS.

CONTENTS.

The outline sketch on p. 115 is a tracing from Stieler's "*Iran und Turan*," 1891. The other three sketch maps are engraved from a reduction of the Map of Afghanistan, published at Calcutta in 1889, which, in spite of the dates, is more recent, and differs materially from Stieler's sheet.

IMPERIAL DEFENCE.

INTRODUCTION.

An enquirer into the nature and sufficiency of
the preparation of the British Empire for war
is confronted by a preliminary difficulty. The
suffering entailed on man by every international conflict, the suspicion that wars have
too often been entered upon without justification or without a clear understanding of the
purposes to be served by them, and the growth
of a human sympathy which rightly shrinks
from every form of violence, have given rise
to a widespread feeling that war is wicked in
itself, and might perhaps, by political arrangement, be rendered unnecessary. Many of our
countrymen, accordingly, abstain from all

enquiry into the principles of naval and military administration, believing that the discussion of these questions promotes the growth of a militant disposition, and thereby increases the evil which they wish to avoid. We propose, therefore, to set out with some examination of this belief, and to explain our conviction that the maintenance of an adequate and well-organised naval and military force is a national necessity and a national duty. Nothing short of this conviction would justify us in submitting to our countrymen the enquiry which forms the substance of this book.

Cobden, in his first work, ' England, Ireland, and America,' published in 1835, expressed the opinion that " at some future election we may probably see the test of ' *no foreign politics* ' applied to those who offer to become the representatives of free constituencies." The great services which Cobden rendered to the state have given weight to all his utterances,

and this passage, which comes in the course
of an argument deprecating intervention in
continental affairs, has been widely remem-
bered, perhaps without sufficient recollection
of its context. The phrase is a loose one, and
its employment by Cobden was unfortunate,
for it gave rise to the impression which is still
common, that wisdom in these matters consists
in having no foreign policy at all. Let us see
what this implies. By a policy we mean a
principle or a purpose applied to or maintained in the conduct of affairs. "No foreign
policy" means, therefore, either that we are
to have no relations with other countries, or
that, having such relations, we are to conduct them without system. But for a nation
of traders to have no dealings with others
would be suicide, and to have dealings without any clear idea of what we are about
is hardly wise. Cobden quoted on his title-
page a saying by George Washington: "The
great rule of conduct for us in regard to

foreign nations is, in extending our commercial relations, to have with them as little *political* connexion as possible." In other words, our traders are to go everywhere and do business all the world over, but our government is to have no more dealings with other governments than are absolutely necessary. This leaves us still in doubt as to what degree of intercourse and intimacy with other governments is a necessity to a nation whose ships are in every port, and whose merchants do the largest share of trade wherever in the wide world trade is carried on.

Trade requires at both ends of its line the protection of law and the security of settled order. So imperious is this need that where European traders have to do with savages the invariable result is the establishment of a form of government among the natives. The whole history of the African coasts illustrates this need, and the history of all the great trading companies shows that mercantile corporations trading with unsettled countries have been compelled to undertake the government of their customers. The trader needs, in the country where he buys and sells, the protection of government. In a civilised and friendly country he enjoys the same security for person and property as he has at home. The laws of the foreign country protect and enforce his contracts, and if the countenance of the foreign government were withdrawn from him, his business would be at an end. Accordingly, civilised governments, so long as they are friendly, reciprocally accord to one another's subjects the benefits they confer upon their own.

Trade intimacy has only gradually become close. In the earlier stages of commerce and of international relations a man had nowhere any rights outside his own country. Governments have by slow degrees created the intricate network of ties by which they are connected. Two nations can thus

become closely intertwined almost without
being conscious of it. Take, for an example,
the connection between England and Germany. A vast trade is done between the
two countries. Great numbers of Germans
are settled in England and of Englishmen
in Germany. Every summer thousands of
tourists cross the separating seas. Inter-
marriages between Germans and English
are of everyday occurrence. The Germans
read our novels and we read their scientific
books. All these things are rendered possible
only by the joint action of the two governments. Commercial treaties, extradition
treaties, copyright treaties protect and extend
private relations ; and a small army of consuls
and diplomatists are busy facilitating the
arrangement of all sorts of possible misunder-
standings. If some impassable wall could be
suddenly raised between the two countries,
there would ensue untold suffering and loss
to each.

Our relations with other nations and other governments are of a similar kind, and their termination would bring about heavy sacrifices on each side. It might, therefore, be wise to substitute for Washington's maxim one that better accords with modern policy, and to say that it is the duty of a government to cultivate such relations with other governments as will conduce to the freest intercourse between the subjects of both, so that the subjects of each shall, as far as possible, have the benefits they would enjoy if they were at the same time subjects of both.

The true basis for a continuance of these intimate international relations is the general recognition of the advantage arising from them. From partial identity or mutuality of interests arises a common purpose, and a joint action or agreement between the two governments expressed in the various treaties and arrangements subsisting between them.

There may, however, be a divergence of interests, real or supposed, which will carry with it a loosening of the tie, and which may even so far prevail as to outweigh or to obscure the advantages of co-operation. It may take the shape of a direct opposition of interests, so that the two parties may come into conflict with one another. In that case the task of restoring the community of purpose devolves upon the two governments. Where the interests at stake are of subordinate importance, a settlement is effected by concession, by compromise, or by arbitration. Is there not, however, a point beyond which the state cannot go in compromise or concession? A state may make every concession compatible with its own existence, that is, with a proper performance of its own functions; but it cannot surrender its existence or abandon its work. What then, in the last resort, is the specific function of the state; the purpose for which it exists? The state represents the common good of its citizens. It is the basis of their higher life. It secures to its subjects the only possibility for the exercise—for the full development—of their faculties. It supplies them with the ideal aim of a common good. It may continue to exist so long as its individuality and its independence are maintained. But, no nation can submit, without self-effacement, to the orders of another. The first duty of a state is to preserve its own free-will, and in its dealings with other states to maintain at least a formal respect for their sovereignty.

When, in 1870, the crown of Spain was provisionally offered to a Hohenzollern prince, and the French government communicated to that of Prussia its objections to the choice, there was nothing improper in such communication, for which, indeed, precedent could be found. The reply that the prince had with drawn his candidature was, however, sufficient. The further demand of the French government that the King of Prussia should promise for the future not to allow any similar candidature was not unnaturally interpreted in Germany as an attempt at dictation, that is, as an affront to the sovereignty of Prussia. If the object desired had been a settlement in accordance with French susceptibilities, of the succession to the Spanish crown, it could have been obtained by friendly negotiation.

The possibility of conflict, the fact that we may at any moment be confronted with the obligation to stake our existence in order to preserve our spiritual integrity, is not removed by refusing to perceive it, and applies no less to the nation than to the individual. A community does not sacrifice or modify its political and social institutions in deference to a wish from outside. To challenge these institutions is to provoke a conflict. And such a challenge can perhaps not always be declined.

The growth of the United States of America was accompanied by the development, due

to soil, climate, and other conditions, of
two contradictory systems of society. The
mark of the Northern States was industrial
activity. In the Southern States, the whole
social system rested upon, and was bound up
with, the institution of slavery. To each of
these systems alike expansion was a necessity,
but the expansion of either must be a restraint
upon that of the other. The civil war could
have been avoided only if one side or the
other could have voluntarily agreed to the
abolition of the institutions and to the nega-
tion of the ideals with which its existence
appeared to be bound up. It is easy to say
now that slavery was a wrong, and that it was,
therefore, the duty of the South to abandon it
without a quarrel. To the Southerners who
fought for it, it seemed justified, and it was
the point upon which all their interests
centred — the condition of their material
prosperity.

No nation willingly parts either from its

traditions or from its prospects. Where the
traditions of one bar the prospects of another,
a conflict is almost inevitable. Such a case
was that of Germany in the years before the
war of 1866. The treaties of 1815 had
denied to Germany that national existence
which was recognised by its people as a supreme need. The constitution made by the
Congress left Prussia and Austria rival clai-
mants for the leading influence in a confederation of impotent principalities. Yet both
Prussia and Austria were great states, neither
of which could be expected to submit to dictation from outside. Austria was half in and
half out of Germany, and was bent upon using
her predominance in the confederation for
the promotion of Austrian, that is, of non-
German, aims. In these aims it was difficult
for Prussia as a purely German state to con-
cur, and accordingly the very constitution of
the confederation involved a struggle between
these two powers for the right to direct its

policy. Prussia could not avoid the conflict
without a self-effacement which implied de-
spair of her future, and Austria could not
abandon her claim to the leadership of Germany without such a break with her past as
no healthy state will contemplate.

It is no part of our purpose to make an ex-
haustive analysis of the possible causes of war.
It is enough that conflict is sometimes inevitable, and that the conditions which make it
so may have their roots in healthy forms of
national growth. The path of duty, however,
will not be found by an exclusive attention to
material interests. This is rather the sphere
in which concession is usually easy and reasonable. But no nation can afford to part with
its spiritual birthright, for it can do so only
with the loss of all that makes its nationality
worth having. We are accustomed to regard
as the type of moral perfection the character
which prefers death to the abandonment of
an ideal of duty. Sir Thomas More, Catholic

though he was, is a hero for most Protestant Englishmen. If we are right in approving in the case of the individual man or woman the maxim " death before dishonour," it can hardly be right in the conduct of national affairs to adopt a mere calculation of commercial or material interests. The condition of moral strength that " Whosoever will save his life shall lose it," applies not to the individual alone, but to the nation.

The conclusion that the use of force may be necessary in the last resort, even in pursuit of righteous ends, comes out clearly from an analogy often appealed to in support of the opposite view. In private life we take no consideration for our defence. Our security depends on the policeman, and on the fact that behind him lie all the resources of the state. So complete is the protection thus afforded, and so permanent, that we never dream of the employment of force to influence the conduct of others. Yet the conflict of wills is constant and continuous. Each of us has his purposes, to the fulfilment of which his energies are constantly bent. The condition of their pursuit is that the rights of others shall be respected. In this absence of private violence we are accustomed to see the fundamental distinction between the civilised and the savage state. No one supposes the desires of the civilised man to be less numerous or less imperious than those of the savage. But in a civilised community, the forces which savages waste in indiscriminate conflict are made subservient to the common good. The state declares war against wrong-doers, against those who refuse to recognise the common good, and for their suppression has in reserve an unlimited store of violence. It is clearly understood that the state will use violence only to assert the common good as it is re-cognised by the explicit and formal sanction of the law. Subject to this condition, the state may in the last resort command the bodily exertions of all its subjects for the suppression of evil-doers; and if this vast capital of force is not called up, it is only because it forms the basis of an unlimited credit.

If we can suppose the state to abolish itself, and the community to dissolve partnership, it is evident that all our security would be gone, and that every man would have to depend for the protection of his person and the retention of his property upon his own courage and strength. The condition of each individual man upon this supposition corresponds very closely with that of every independent nation in its relations with the rest of the world.

The inference has been drawn from this analogy that progress is to be expected from the organisation of states into a higher form of community, towards which they would stand in a relation similar to that of the individual citizen to the state. From this development, it is thought, the ideal of a universal peace may ultimately be attained. A single government, the representative of a common good recognised by all mankind, would control the militant energies of the whole race for the suppression of those who were unable to accept that common good. The peace of the world would rest, as the Queen's peace now rests, upon the credit produced by the existence of an infinite stock of violence. The capital would perhaps never be called up, and for working purposes only an infinitesimal percentage would be required.

That the ideal of a world-state and of universal peace is acceptable is not here either asserted or denied. It is at the best an ideal for the distant future. It has been touched upon as an illustration of the truth that order in the largest sense—the practical enjoyment of rights—is rendered possible by a perpetual threat to restrain by violence those who would disturb it. There are no doubt those who

c

will shrink from the admission that our civilisation and its highest possibilities for spiritual
growth at present rest upon a perpetual readiness to fight. Their feeling, however, can
hardly be a healthy one, for it is a protest
against the unalterable condition of human
life, the existence of evil. It is only the
weak, sick man who deplores his liability to
temptation. The sound man fights his battles,
if need be, and in the long-run wins them.
Sentimentality is a convenient cloak for a
great deal of lax thought and moral weakness.
If there is no more noble character than the
strong man who under bitter insult and wrong
is constrained by a high sense of duty to turn
his cheek to the smiter, there is none so contemptible as the coward who endeavours
to conceal his impotence by parading his
humility.

According to this view, the act of carrying
on war is not in itself either good or bad. It
becomes right or wrong according as the object

with which it is undertaken is just or unjust. Unless this were the case the profession of a soldier would be in itself degrading. Yet it has never been regarded as other than an honourable calling except by the sentimental school of our own day, which nowhere exposes its looseness of thought more clearly than in this connection. Its disciples speak of soldiers, or rather of most soldiers, for they make exceptions—Gordon, for example—as men whose business is to kill, and appear to suppose that this settles the question. But the characteristic mark of the soldier is not that he kills, but that he perpetually exposes himself to being killed. And this risk is not, as in the case of the doctor, a mere slight increase, incidental to his profession, of the ordinary risks of life, but is the fundamental element of his professional duty. Moreover, when the soldier does kill, the act is entirely devoid of personal malice, which constitutes the criminal characteristic of murder. For besides and beyond the danger which is the pervading atmosphere of the soldier's calling, must be considered the obedience which has an equal claim with bravery to be the special military virtue. The fact that he acts in obedience to orders relieves the soldier, as such, from responsibility for the policy on behalf of which he fights.   It is the statesman who is responsible for a war, and the statesman will always be pronounced guiltless if his policy was just, and if in its pursuit the recourse to arms was inevitable.

It seems then that war should be conceived of as imposed upon states by an irreconcilable opposition of purposes.   It is analogous to litigation in private life, and, like litigation, is appealed to only in the last resort.   In the one case as in the other the issue of the contest is uncertain, the expense is heavy, and the probability that the loser will have to pay the costs is an inducement to prefer any other possible means of settlement.

The recourse to arms is thus always a means to an end. This apparently commonplace conclusion is neither so obvious nor so unimportant as might appear, for it has often been forgotten by statesmen and governments, and always with disastrous consequences. The Eastern war of 1854–55 was undertaken by the Allies with very little clearness of thought. In its earlier portion they had a definite purpose, to compel Russia to abandon the Danubian principalities. When the principalities had been evacuated this object was attained, and Turkey was secure. The expedition to the Crimea had no definite political purpose. Its originators fancied that the destruction of Sebastopol would be a humiliation to Russia. It may be doubted whether this object, unsatisfactory in itself, was actually attained. Russia had rendered herself contemptible by her miserable failure on the Danube. The attack on Sebastopol saved her honour by giving the opportunity for a stubborn and glorious defence, and at the first subsequent favourable conjuncture the destruction was repaired and the Black Sea clause repudiated. It is difficult now to avoid the impression that the attack on Sebastopol was a fight for the sake of fighting, and that the reasons which have been alleged in its justification are *ex post facto* attempts to connect it with a rational policy.

The French Court in July, 1870, seems to have picked a quarrel in order to bring on a war. The flimsiness of the main pretext has already been discussed. The opening acts of the campaign prove that the real advisers of Louis Napoleon had no plan except to take their army to the frontier and await a collision. No doubt this secured what they wanted; but if they had had a definite political end they would have considered the means of attaining it, and would, therefore, have learned enough about the Prussian army to prevent them from raising a quarrel until they had remodelled their own forces.

An almost exactly similar case is that of King Milan's Government in 1885. The union of the two parts of Bulgaria had caused in Servia a jealousy precisely like that aroused in France by the union of Germany. The Serbs, like the French, conceived the wish to humiliate their neighbours, and, with an un-ready army and without a plan, proceeded to attack them.

These instances perhaps sufficiently show the folly of war for its own sake. Like all other folly it is based on confusion of thought, and in each of these cases would have been avoided if the responsible statesman had realised that war is a means and cannot be an end in itself.

Not less irrational, but much more com-mon, is the belief that the avoidance of war is an end in itself. It can be secured only by con-cession or compromise, and where the purpose is the maintenance of a fundamental right or the protection of a vital interest, concession or compromise is an irreparable injury to the character of the nation which agrees to it.

This kind of injury can perhaps best be made clear from a somewhat analogous case in ordinary life. A young man while at the university decides, from deep conviction, to devote his life to the good of his fellows as a clergyman. He takes orders and throws himself heart and soul into his work. As time goes on he marries and becomes the father of a family. But as his spiritual and intellectual growth proceeds, and his grasp of life enlarges, his views undergo a transformation of which he is at first hardly aware. The time comes when he discovers that the particular symbols of faith which he conscientiously adopted in earlier years are incompatible with his now mature convictions. He has, therefore, to choose between his conscience and his living, between social and spiritual ruin.

The ever-present possibility of such a conflict between two duties is the tragic condition of life from which there is no escape. It is veiled from our everyday consciousness because, though material distress is palpable to all, the outside observer can rarely see the deterioration that results from moral failure. Yet there must be many who know the bitter experience, *propter vitam vivendi perdere causas.*

The recent negotiations with France concerning the so-called French Shore in Newfoundland well illustrate the dangers that arise from supposing peace to be an end in itself. The French have an undoubted right to fish in the territorial waters of half the Newfoundland coast, and to make temporary landings for the purpose of drying fish. Ever since 1714 the French have from time to time claimed an exclusive right to fish in these waters, a claim which the British government has invariably denied. The efforts of France to assert this claim, and the consequent danger of collisions between French and British subjects, have led to repeated but hitherto fruitless negotiations. An agreement reached in 1885 between the two governments failed to secure acceptance by the colonists, and never acquired validity. Thereupon the French government, by way of pushing its own view of the contested rights, declared an intention to extend its protection to French subjects who should in future undertake the " exploitation of the lobster." The British government protested against the erection of French lobster factories as an infringement of the treaties.   In March 1890 a *modus vivendi* for one year, afterwards prolonged for a second year, was agreed upon between the two governments, by which the French existing lobster factories are provisionally tolerated, while no new English ones can be undertaken ; and in March 1891 an arbitration upon the French claim with regard to the catching and preparation of lobsters was agreed upon, with a proviso that the arbitrators might afterwards deal with other subsidiary questions. The colonists protest against the arbitration as implying the entertainment of an altogether unfounded French claim, and against the *modus vivendi* as likely, by its provisional acceptance of the existing, but as they and the British government contend, illegal French factories, to prejudice the arbitrators in favour of the claim. These concessions, and the remarkable readiness of the government to meet halfway a Power which is, by its own admission, trying to make the most of an at least doubtful case, were defended by Lord Knutsford, who said : " If the French insisted on their claims, the question could only be settled by war, and this country might be assured that war would not be sanctioned in such a question until after diplomacy had said its last word." Lord Kimberley expressed approval of Lord Knutsford's language.

This doctrine amounts to an abdication of rights in consequence of a threat. The prin-

ciple which it involves is that the British
government will consent to arbitration upon
any claims the refusal of which might conceivably lead to war.   But this principle is
not consistently adopted by the government,
for the conduct of the dispute with Portugal
shows that it is not from war as a wicked
thing that the government shrinks, but from
war as a dangerous thing.   A war with
Portugal might be risked, but not a war
with France.

It seems, therefore, that the policy which
makes peace its prime end is founded not
upon justice, but upon fear.   The Newfound-
landers, though no doubt their irritation has
led to extreme and unjustifiable utterances,
cannot be blamed for drawing the inference
either that Great Britain has lost the will to
defend her rights, or that Newfoundland is not
considered an integral portion of the Empire.

The essential point, however, lies deeper.
It is not merely that there are objects more

desirable than peace, but that peace cannot be secured by a policy which adopts it as a supreme end. The partial admission of the French claims just discussed only strengthens the position of the French government for further demands ; and if it were true, which it is not, that the French government was prepared to press its claim to the point of actual conflict, the process already gone through must be repeated again and again. There can be no limit to the concessions which must be made to avoid a quarrel, for whenever the point comes at which concession is refused, the quarrel will be there. Either the French government took up the question in order to provoke a quarrel, or its object was to extend as far as possible the industrial opportunities of a class of its subjects. If a quarrel was intended, the concessions made by Great Britain avail her nothing—a new pretext can at any moment be found. If the object was to benefit the French fisheries, the French

government adopted a proper and natural
course. To have raised a claim and at the
same time to have announced that they were
not prepared to support it by an appeal to
arms, would have been to declare beforehand
that the claim was not seriously meant. It
was for the English statesman to consider
whether the rights claimed by France represented either a material interest of such
magnitude as to be worth to that country the
gigantic effort of a war, or such a vital and
necessary right as France could not afford to
forego. The answer to these questions must
have shown either that the claims would be
dropped, or an offer of general arbitration
made as soon as they were seriously refused,
and that any real intention to press them to
an open quarrel could exist only if there was
a purpose, independent of them, to force a
war upon Great Britain.

A true statesman, then, according to the
view we have put forward, will always have

positive aims, not seeking a quarrel for its own sake, and avoiding unnecessary disputes, but not shrinking from resistance whenever the individuality of the nation or its right to do its own work in the world is threatened.

The necessity and the justice of a task should be ascertained before it is undertaken. A nation cannot lightly embark in an enterprise and afterwards lightly resign it, without laying itself open to the charge of frivolity. It is, therefore, at the inception of a policy that the question whether it may or may not involve collision with other Powers, or the ultimate employment of force, should be considered. In other words, the question of peace or war should be examined not merely at the moment when a conflict of purposes becomes a quarrel, but at the moment when a policy which may involve conflict is adopted.

For example, the Salisbury-Waddington agreement to maintain the Khedive's govern-

ment in Egypt, and the Granville-Gambetta
note of January 1882 to the same effect, implied
the intention to suppress by force any such
revolt as that of 1882. This was clearly understood by both Cabinets. When, therefore, the
French Chamber refused to vote money for the
expedition, they were drawing back from a
policy previously adopted. This is always a
dangerous step, for it shakes the self-confidence of a nation, and the French have never
ceased to regret their decision. Mr. Bright
made a similar mistake by remaining in the
Cabinet while the policy was accepted, and
resigning only when the time came to carry it
into action. If Mr. Bright thought intervention in itself wrong, he should have been no
party to a policy which implied such action
in certain, not improbable, contingencies. If
he held that the policy could be carried out
without recourse to violence, he should have
suggested the alternative. To embark on a
policy without having considered the conse-

quences is to prepare for ourselves the position of Lot's wife.

It is impossible to dwell too strongly upon the folly and the wickedness of an aggressive war—that is, of a war undertaken with the intention of encroachment upon the just rights or interference with the legitimate undertakings of another nation. It is equally impossible to doubt the right of a nation to resist to the uttermost an unprovoked or wanton attack. But it is only by a confusion of thought that the moral approval or condemnation accorded to a policy can be extended to the form of the military operations—attack and defence. Our moral judgment of a policy may largely depend upon its aggressive or its conservative character. But no moral judgment whatever attaches to a military operation from the fact that it constitutes attack or defence. In the actual conduct of war attack and defence perpetually alternate with one another, and there is no such thing as an attack which does not

D

change into defence, or a defence which does
not from time to time pass into attack. The
army or the fleet which is able to take the
offensive invariably attacks, and the force
which acts for the time on the defensive does
so only in order to gain a better opportunity
for attack. The motto of the English Volunteers—" Defence, not Defiance "—is the ex-
pression of sound political feeling : as a military maxim it is nonsense. If there is one
point upon which professional soldiers and
sailors are unanimous, it is that in the long
run the only effective defence consists in
attack, and the highest ideal of defensive
generalship is an action in which the defender
delays his attack until the adversary is ex-
hausted.

The confusion between defence as a political
attitude and defence as an operation of war
has had disastrous consequences. It has led
to the neglect by English public opinion of all
naval and military preparations that might be

available for attack, and to a preference for
the means of passive defence. Forts, because
they cannot be moved against an enemy, and
the Volunteers, because they are not available
for foreign service, have enjoyed a popularity
denied to the regular army, which is regarded
as the possible instrument of an aggressive
policy. The results have been a large expenditure upon forts, some of which are of
doubtful value for any probable war, and a
style of training for the Volunteers which, as
it does not fit them to take the field, renders
them as helpless for defence at home as they
are supposed to be for attack abroad. But
the essential elements of combative strength
are mobile. Fleets and armies can move from
place to place, and it is upon their exertions
that victory ultimately rests. Fixed defences,
whether protecting from attack by sea or by
land, are mere supports and auxiliaries to the
action of armies and fleets. Thus, the vital
element of defensive strength is from its nature

equally available for offensive operations, and no efficient preparation for defence is possible that will not also serve for attack.

The traditional anathema upon foreign affairs has been largely due to the same erroneous ideas. Its legacy has been the long prevalent indifference of the public towards the organisation of our maritime protection. The course of continental affairs and the growth of the Volunteer force has brought about a widespread interest in all that concerns land warfare ; but the nature and conditions of maritime war, upon which, after all, the security of Great Britain and of her Empire mainly depends, have been left to professional students whose work, in the absence of the invigorating support of general interest and sympathy, has been, until within the last two or three years, somewhat barren of result.

The attempt which has been made to illustrate the nature of war, and its relations to policy, has thus a direct practical purpose. Without a clear and a true conception of the character of war as a conflict of national purposes, the proper conduct of military operations and of defensive preparations is impossible. The present unorganised condition of the defence of the British Empire is due far more to the prevalence of misconceptions in regard to these elementary and fundamental truths, than to the lack of honest endeavour on the part of those who are directly responsible.

We may now turn our eyes from general principles to the particular case before us—the defence of the British Empire. We think we may safely assume that Englishmen, wherever they live, will lay down their lives, if need be, to protect English homes, both those of the Old Country and of the New Englands beyond the seas; that they will fight in defence of the work of peace and good government which has been undertaken in India;

and last, but not least, that they will never
abandon without a struggle the command of
the sea, which alone renders possible their
trade, their insular security, and their Empire.

CHAPTER I.

THE PRIMACY OF THE NAVY.

THE character of the British Empire will be found by tracing its distribution over the world. It follows everywhere the margin of the ocean. British settlements and British authority are planted at intervals all along the coast of Africa; they are dotted all round the shores of the Indian Ocean. Most of the islands, great and small, are covered by the British flag. Even where strong and civilised Powers, as old or older than the English nation, might seem able to secure their coasts from the salt-water incrustation, British influence has penetrated. On both coasts of Europe

the small islands are or have been British.
The Englishman has sat down at the gates
of the Celestial Empire.   Where two seas
meet, or where a double coast-line makes
a land peculiarly accessible to influences
from the sea, this sea-borne energy seems
more than usually potent.   Witness the long
possession of Gibraltar and the steady progress of British power in India and in South
Africa.   It is as though the sea had been
saturated with British influence, and had
deposited it along all the unprotected portion
of its margin.

This is something more than a mere figure
of speech.   It is a statement of fact.   From
the time of the Dutch wars of the 17th century
the population of the surface of the sea has
been predominantly British, and this predominance once established has so increased
that at the present moment one-half of the
tonnage of the world is British, no other single
nation possessing a tenth.   The predominance

is much more striking, however, in the case of the most active part of the world's marine—the steamers. The gross tonnage of steamers in the world in 1888 slightly exceeded ten millions, of which nearly seven millions of tons were British, while no other nation owned a million tons. It is evident that a crowd containing seventy Englishmen, seven Frenchmen, six Germans, five Americans, one or two Italians, two or three Spaniards, a Dutchman, a Norwegian, a Swede, and a Dane, is, for all practical purposes, an English crowd; and such a crowd would accurately represent the nationality of the steamers in the world. The ocean is, in fact, a British possession, not indeed a British property conveyed and settled by treaties or title deeds, but English in the sense that Englishmen incomparably more than any others use it and occupy it. Wherever ships touch English is spoken. At every landing-place in the world, where no civilised power is supreme, the English

language, British trade, and British influence
are paramount. And, had it not been
that for nearly fifty years British Governments refused to increase their responsibilities,
all the uncivilised coasts in the world
would have long ago been under British
protection.

The British Empire, in short, is the possession of the sea. So long as the state of things
just described continues, all countries must be
pervaded by British influence in proportion as
they are accessible by sea. While this condition lasts the Empire cannot be irreparably
harmed. This British ocean life needs only a
nucleus to swiftly form a settlement, a colony,
or even an empire. Cut off from the sea, not
one of our colonies, not one of our dependencies could prosper. From it they, like
ourselves, derive their nourishment and their
strength.

Let us suppose that this ocean life were
stopped. Suppose the whole salt sea to

become suddenly frozen, or to be transformed
into a desert of shifting sands. The British
Empire would that moment perish. Great
Britain, indeed, and the more healthy among
her colonies, might continue to exist, but it
would be as separate nations, unconnected
with one another, and each dependent entirely
upon its own resources, or upon such exchange
as might be possible across the sands or ice
with neighbouring countries.

Again, suppose that the sea, instead of
being frozen or being changed into a Sahara,
received some mysterious constitution which
made it unable to bear on its surface a
British ship, while it retained for the ships
of other nations all its navigable qualities.
The British Empire would, as before, have
ceased to exist, and its several parts would
fall an easy prey to whichever of the remaining sea-going nations should be disposed
to attack them. Each colony left to itself,
unable to be succoured from home or from

the neighbouring colonies, would have to depend for its defence on its own unaided resources. The hypothesis just made seems wild and impossible—the ocean cannot be frozen ; the salt water cannot become a sandy desert. But there are conditions by no means impossible under which the ocean might become to all intents impassable by British ships. This would be the case during a war in which the British fleets should have been defeated and compelled to seek the refuge of their fortified harbours. There would then be no protection for British ships at sea. A less degree of danger, though no small one, would exist during a war in which the hostile fleets, even though not victorious, should succeed in evading those of Great Britain. If, however, the hostile fleets were shut up in their own ports, British merchant ships would enjoy comparative safety. Hostile cruisers would no doubt scour the seas. But their ravages could be kept within tolerable limits by a judicious system of convoys, and by a proper employment of British cruisers to intercept and capture or destroy the raiders.

It becomes clear, then, that the first point at which the British Empire is vulnerable is in its sea-borne life, and that the repulse of an attack upon our maritime industry must be entirely the work of the Navy. If the Navy had no other function, this duty alone would give it supreme importance for national defence.

The second conceivable form of attack is an invasion of some British territory— either of Great Britain, or of some colony, or of India. An invasion, except that of India by Russia, or of Canada by the United States, is possible only by sea. In this case also, therefore, the Navy must play a prominent part.

The fact that the sea is, so to speak, all road carries with it the consequence that any fleet is liable to be attacked sooner or later by

any hostile fleet afloat anywhere, the prox-
imity of the danger at any moment being
measured by the distance which separates the
two. No fleet can therefore be secure against
interruption in any operation, such as the
transport or landing of troops, or a territorial
attack, which requires a longer time than is
represented by the distance of the nearest
hostile fleet.

If, therefore, it is intended to undertake
and carry out in security any particular
operation, such as a landing, the force
so engaged must be protected by a force
devoted to resisting any hostile attempt at
interruption. Suppose the object to be the
capture of an island. If no hostile fleet
exists, the capture can be assured by transporting to and landing on the island a military
force strong enough to overcome any local
resistance. If a hostile fleet is within reach,
the attempt cannot safely be made. The
hostile fleet must first be disposed of. The

safest plan would be first to destroy the hostile fleet, and then to commence the transport of troops to the island. A very great superiority of force, and a certainty of finding the hostile fleet, would perhaps justify a separation of forces; one part being detailed to watch, delay, or destroy the hostile fleet, while the other part conducted the operations against the island. The problem is the same whatever the size or the distance of the island, the varying factor being the amount of force necessary to overcome the local resistance. If the hostile fleet be far away, and the garrison of the island small, the place may be captured before the enemy's fleet can interfere; but tenure will be precarious, and can only be made secure by the defeat of the fleet which might contest it.

In other words, an attack on land conducted across the sea is a most hazardous speculation so long as there exists anywhere a hostile fleet that is able to fight. In

order to make such an attack safe, it is
indispensable that the attacker should secure
himself from all interruption by destroying or
driving from the sea any hostile fleet. The
Power which should succeed in doing this
would have "the command of the sea" as
against its particular enemy, and could then
undertake in any part of the sea any operations desired.

The command of the sea, then, means
the possession of an invincible fleet which
has gained so decisive a victory, or series
of victories, as to render hopeless any renewal of the struggle against it. The territories of the Power having the command of
the sea are virtually safe against attack by
the sea, and the territories of a Power which
possesses any fighting fleet at all are unlikely
to be attacked until its fleet has been defeated
or destroyed. Any Power aiming at attack
upon territory across the sea must endeavour
first to obtain command of the sea, that is, to

destroy the fleets of its enemy, and any operations against territory undertaken without this preliminary will be hazardous and uncertain.

The British Navy, then, so long as it maintains the superiority at sea, is a sufficient protection against invasion for every part of the Empire except India and Canada. If, however, the Navy were to suffer decisive defeat, if it were driven to seek the shelter of its fortified harbours and kept there, or if it were destroyed, then, not only would every part of the Empire be open to invasion, but the communications between the several parts would be cut, and no mutual succour would be possible.

The defeat of the British fleet or fleets would of course be effected by purely naval operations; but the acquiescence in its destruction could, perhaps, only be secured by a blow affecting the British power at its source, and therefore, the establishment by an enemy

E

of his naval superiority, would almost certainly
be followed by an invasion of Great Britain.
So long then as the British Navy can be
maintained invincible, the Empire would be
adequately defended against the attack of any
European Power other than Russia, and for
such a defence, therefore, no more is needed
than complete naval preparation and such
military preparation as is required for the
full efficiency of the Navy. Any additional
military preparation is, as against attack of
this nature, merely an insurance to cover the
possibility of the failure of the Navy. After
such failure, it might save the British Islands,
but it could not save the Empire.

A different problem again would arise in the
case of an attack by Russia aiming at the
conquest of India, or an attack by the United
States aiming at the conquest of Canada. In
either of these cases, the enemy being best able
to approach by land would not necessarily
require to wrest from us the command of the

sea, and if Canada or India were strong enough
to defend itself against the United States or
Russia, the command of the sea would not
be necessary for their defence. But neither
Canada, nor even India in the long run, is
strong enough ; and, therefore, for their defence
they require uninterrupted communication with
the rest of the Empire, so that the command
of the sea is in these cases also a necessity for
Great Britain.

Neither Russia nor the United States is
likely to be able in any future which need at
present be considered to enter into a maritime contest with Great Britain. It would
be the policy of either Government to obtain
the co-operation of a maritime Power for this
purpose. Superiority at sea would be as
indispensable for Great Britain as ever, and
would be combined with the necessity for
superiority on land. The case of the United
States may, it is hoped, be dismissed as improbable, and for practical purposes the cases to

be considered reduce themselves to three : a war with France (about Egypt, or Siam, or Newfoundland, or some other of the dangerous questions often pending between the Western Powers), which would turn primarily upon the question of naval supremacy ; a war with Russia, which would be a land war for the defence of India ; or a combination including both these wars at once.

There is a preliminary question of the gravest import which a foreign statesman, before embarking on such a contest, must answer for himself, and which Great Britain, therefore, cannot reasonably leave unsettled. What is the power with which, in case of conflict, our enemy would have to contend ? Is it Great Britain, or is it the British Empire ?

No doubt a war with Great Britain is, technically speaking, also a war with the British Empire ; but the question is whether in such a struggle the British Government would be able to draw only on the resources of the United

Kingdom or of the United Kingdom and India, or whether they would be able to throw into the scale all the energy and all the resources of every part of the Queen's dominions. Great Britain alone, though no doubt her resources are equal, if not superior, to those of any other European nation, has yet no such undoubted superiority of wealth and of energy as to make unreasonable the idea of attacking her, or the expectation of a possible victory against her. But the resources of the British Empire are so vast, that if it were believed that they would be fully and freely employed, and were reasonably organised for defence, no statesman of any nation would in his sober senses dream of provoking a conflict single-handed.

This belief, unfortunately, can hardly be said to exist. Opposite views on this subject flourish side by side. Some people seem to think that it is the business of Great Britain out of her own resources to defend the Empire against all comers. The other

and the more logical doctrine is, that every
subject of the Queen is in the last resort
bound to assist in the defence of any and
every part of the Queen's dominions.   Even
thus, however, there would remain a doubt
as to whether he in fact can be counted on
to do so.   The question, besides its military
aspect, has other bearings which it is impossible
here fully to examine.   It is enough to say, that
the great question, perhaps the greatest question which has to be answered by the present
generation of Englishmen, is whether the
British Empire is to become a series of independent, though, perhaps, friendly states, or to
make a reality of the military unity which at
the present time is rather a sentiment than a
practical institution.

It is evidently impossible to organise the
defences of the Empire until this prior question has been settled, and it is quite impossible until it has been faced to determine
properly the policy of Great Britain.   If the

principle of the unity of the Empire and of the unity of its defences is maintained, the greatest conceivable degree of security would have been gained for the whole and for every part, and the British Empire could afford, as against the attack of any single Power, to steer clear of all alliances, and to pursue a policy directed solely to the immediate welfare of its subjects. If, on the other hand, the unity of defence is imperilled, it might in the long run seem necessary for Great Britain, saddled as she must be with the task of defending India, to seek to relieve herself by the assistance of a Continental alliance, and to modify her policy in such a manner as to secure that object.

Before, then, the defence of the British Empire can be placed throughout on a permanently satisfactory footing, it seems necessary that the great political question of the century should be settled, and that Englishmen all over the world should make up their minds as to the real nature of Greater Britain.

The old view that the colonies were so many possessions of Great Britain, to be regarded as sources of profit or of power to the mother country, has been abandoned, and cannot be revived. Instead of it, two alternatives are offered. The one involves the collapse of British power, and if it is accepted will leave Great Britain herself and each of her colonies independent indeed, but deprived of all the advantages of mutual aid for protection and progress. The other, which we hope will prevail, asserts that there is one England, not confined to these islands, maintaining, wherever Englishmen are settled, the same ideals and the same traditions, and developing in a Greater Britain the liberty and respect for law which have hitherto been the proudest monument of their history.

The possibility that a western rival may one day strike a blow directed against our maritime power, and may aim in the long run at wresting from us some of our colonial

possessions, and the other possibility that
Russia may attempt to supplant us in India,
are more or less familiar to Englishmen.
What has not been sufficiently clearly pre-
sented to English readers is the possible connection between these two rivalries, at first
sight apparently distinct.

The French have never forgotten that our
gain in India was their loss. It was as the
stepping - stone to India that Egypt first
attracted them, and their present interest in
Egypt is not disconnected from the renewal of
their enterprise in the Far East. A Russian
ambition to conquer India would have, therefore, a natural connection with the French
desire to readjust, to the disadvantage of Great
Britain, the balance of power on the northern
shore of the Indian Ocean. As we have seen,
the defence of India against Russian attack
depends for effectiveness on that command of
the sea which alone will enable England to
sustain the energy of her armies. To interrupt

our sea communications with Karachi would be
to paralyse the local defence of India.   Such a
blow to our maritime power would be of the
greatest conceivable assistance to the Russian
design.   Under present conditions it is hardly
conceivable that it could be attempted by any
other Power than France.   Accordingly, for
the purpose of an attack upon India, Russia
has the greatest interest in obtaining the co-
operation of the French.

On the other hand, the prime object
of France in any conflict with Great Britain
must necessarily be to put an end to our
maritime predominance.   It is remarkable
that in the hundred years' maritime conflict
with France, there was only one moment
when England's superiority was doubtful
and when her defeat seemed possible.   It was
when she was engaged at the same time
in a land warfare carried on in a distant
possession.   For, while it was the assistance
of France which enabled the United States

to gain their independence, it was only because the British fleets were hampered by the necessities of the American War that the French and Spaniards were able to recover Minorca and to besiege Gibraltar. A land war in India which England could not evade would therefore offer to France the most favourable opportunity possible for contesting the command of the sea.

It is evident that, assuming in the policies of France and of Russia the possibility of conflict with Great Britain, each of these Powers has a paramount interest in joining hands with the other in the attack, for to each of them such a combination offers the best chance of success. If the combined assault were victorious, there would be an end of the British Empire. India would be lost, and the sea power, which is the life of our Empire, would be broken.

This loss of sea power would leave each of our colonies in a position of isolation, without the guarantee of an assured British future. The lot of French Canada—the loss of its original allegiance—might be reserved for any of them, except, perhaps, Australia. It is this consideration which supplies the all-sufficient motive which should induce the colonies to join heartily in the work of defence, and to submit to the unity of direction, without which war cannot be efficiently conducted.

Some may think that from these considerations there flows a further result. The best way to hamper France in her possible assault on our maritime power would be, they may say, to find her occupation on land. The surest way to prevent the accumulation of Russian forces on the Hari Rud or on the Helmand would be to engage them nearer home. Accordingly, prudence would, perhaps, suggest that England should seek that co-operation with European Powers which has in earlier wars served her in good stead, and which indeed alone made possible the creation of her

Empire. It is impossible to be too strong for defence. The true policy of England is therefore, we may be told, not only to develop and organise the military resources of her Empire as a whole, but to seek the alliance of those Central European Powers whose interests nowhere run counter to her own, and who are anxious and willing to enter into a limited partnership with the mistress of the seas.

In that hopelessness as to the tendency of Australian and Canadian opinion which afflicts British statesmen, such a course might already have been taken were there not a simple but unsurmountable objection. The only purpose we should have in binding ourselves by an alliance would be to induce our allies to fight for our India and for our command of the sea. But it is very unlikely that any allies would do either of these things. That any Continental Power would pledge itself to a war, of which, from the nature of the case, it would have to bear the chief stress, for objects so foreign to its own interests, may well be doubted, and even if the promise were given there could be no certainty that when the time came the Government which had given it would be in a position to fulfil the engagement.

It is impossible wholly to put out of view the fact that Great Britain is a party to certain treaties (such as those which concern the neutrality of Belgium), in defence of which she might possibly be drawn, however unwillingly, to take part in a Continental war.

For such an eventuality no specific preparation is needed beyond what is in any case required to put the defences of the Empire in order. If it became necessary to strike a blow in behalf of the sanctity of a treaty, British action would, in the first instance, take the form of an attack by British fleets upon the enemy's naval power. It is, however, most likely that, once the British Empire has been adequately prepared for defence, a well-

understood intention on the part of its government to fulfil existing pledges of the class
to which we refer would suffice to prevent
infraction of the rights guaranteed.

It is evident that, unless our estimate of
the nature of possible wars is mistaken, the
defence of the Empire rests mainly on the
Navy. So long as the Navy is able to fulfil
its mission, there is little probable scope for
the Army except on the Indian border, or in
offensive operations elsewhere aiming at the
protection of India. Apart from the case of
the defence of India, military operations would
generally be confined to the prevention of a
light attack directed against some naval base.
The use of the Army or of any military force
for defence on land cannot be necessary
against a European enemy until the Navy has
been crushed, that is, until the Empire is on
the verge of destruction. No doubt there
might be occasions when a military expedition
might with advantage be landed on a foreign

coast by way of a counter-stroke, but this
operation is inconceivable except on the hypothesis of a victorious or of an unresisted
Navy. The first result, then, of our enquiry
is to establish in our minds beyond all question the primacy of the Navy in Imperial
defence.

CHAPTER II.

THE COMMAND OF THE SEA.

WE have seen that in any war directed against the British Empire, except a land attack upon India or Canada, the principal work of defence must fall to the Navy. How then must the Navy set about it?

The enemy, whatever the purpose which he intends the war to serve, must necessarily propose to himself to destroy or defeat the Navy. Suppose, in the first instance, that his object is a territorial attack—the conquest either of the British Islands or of any other British possession. He cannot possibly begin the transport of troops until he has reduced the British Navy to a state of hopeless in-

F

feriority.   Admiral Colomb, indeed, in a
lecture delivered on the 1st of March, 1889,
and Professor Laughton, in the course of
the discussion upon it, go so far as to say
that "any commander, if he is wise, will
not undertake a. territorial attack as long as
his operations may be interrupted by a fleet
even considerably weaker than his own ; " and
in his more recent work on 'Naval Warfare,'
Admiral Colomb refers to the operations of
1690 in support of this opinion.   At that time
Lord Torrington, who commanded the English
fleet in the Channel, found himself in presence
of a decidedly superior French force.   Lord
Torrington was of opinion that he ought to
avoid an action, for he said, " If we are beaten,
they, being absolute masters of the sea, will be
at great liberty of doing many things they
dare not attempt whilst we observe them."
He was however compelled, by orders from
London, to risk a battle, in which he was
defeated, but he drew off his fleet before it

was disabled, and retired to the mouth of the Thames. The French made no use of their victory.

We are not entirely convinced by this instance, for there is nothing to show that the French might not have effected a landing by detaching a portion of their fleet to observe Torrington, and covering their transports with the remainder. It seems, therefore, safer to accept the doctrine of Admiral Colomb's ' Naval Warfare' (page 221), that an expedition of magnitude, with an object of attack which requires time to elapse for its reduction, must be protected by a naval force large enough to mask the possibly intercepting naval force, and also a covering force large enough to engage on equal terms any possible fleet which the enemy may bring to bear. In such a case, and in such a case alone, a territorial attack might safely be attempted. This mode of operation would, however, not be possible against Great Britain, except by a very im-

probable combination between the other maritime Powers, until after the British Navy had
suffered a decisive reverse. Accordingly, in the
case under examination, the enemy's objective
must necessarily be, in the first instance, the
British Navy.

The purpose of Great Britain to render
her territories secure would be perfectly
accomplished by the destruction of the
enemy's navy, as this would render any
attempt at the transport of troops impracticable. The destruction of the enemy's navy
would of course also be the best possible
protection for England's sea-borne trade
(though no doubt for this purpose additional
measures would be required), and for her
communications with every part of her Empire. Thus, in every possible war in which
Great Britain could be engaged, the prime
function of the British Navy is to attack,
and, if possible, to destroy the organised
naval forces of the enemy.

But two different methods of carrying on war are open to the enemy.

He may feel strong enough at sea to try to secure for himself that maritime supremacy which for nearly two hundred years has been in the hands of Great Britain. There is abundant evidence that England's sea power is regarded with jealousy by other maritime nations. The manifesto of the allies in 1778 announced their intention " to put an end to that tyrannical empire which England has usurped, and claims to maintain upon the ocean ; " and Jomini lays it down as a desirable principle of European policy, that an unlimited expansion of naval force should not be permitted to any nation which cannot be approached by land. A navy which felt equal to the struggle for the command of the sea would probably seek a decisive battle, and in this case an English commander would have little difficulty in finding his opponents' principal force.

At the present day, however, no navy appears to trust itself thus to throw down the gauntlet to our own. An enemy would probably start with the assumption that his force was inferior, unless, perhaps, in the Mediterranean, and would therefore seek to avoid a battle, except when a fortunate combination might give him the opportunity of attacking with superior numbers an isolated and weaker British fleet. Success in attempts of this kind would largely depend upon evading the English principal force, and the difficulty for a British commander would be to find his enemy and compel him to accept battle.

The surface of the sea, however, while it everywhere offers the same high-road for ships and fleets, retains no tracks after they have passed. If, therefore, an enemy's fleet has once put to sea, it may be exceedingly difficult to ascertain its whereabouts. The only ascertainable point of its course is the starting-point, and therefore the surest way of finding the enemy's fleet is to seek it in one of the ports from which it must start.

At the commencement of the war of 1803, when Lord St. Vincent was First Lord of the Admiralty, his plan at the outset was to place in front of every one of the enemy's military ports a British naval force superior to that which the enemy had within it. In this way the whole French Navy was blockaded. No portion of it could put to sea without the prospect of being immediately attacked by a superior force, and the attempt which might be made by two or more French fleets, evading the watch kept upon them, to unite and attack one of the isolated English blockading fleets, was rendered more dangerous by the fact that Lord St. Vincent kept a reserve fleet in the Channel, ready to reinforce any of the squadrons that might be assailed.

This policy is, perhaps inaccurately, described as that of "blockade." The term is

incorrect, because it does not seem that the
object was in any case to prevent the issue of
the French fleets from their ports, but rather
to prevent their proceeding to sea unwatched,
as by this means several of them might have
combined to attack in superior force an English
detachment.

A plan like this, if it can be carried out,
offers enormous advantages for the defence
of the British Empire. So long as the watch
is kept up, no serious blow can be struck
by the enemy in any part of the world. His
cruisers, no doubt, might escape the vigilance
of our fleets, and attempt to sweep our trade
from the sea. It would therefore be necessary
for Great Britain to have ready, in addition to
the forces employed in the masking operations,
and in addition to the reserve fleet supporting
them, a large number of cruisers for the purpose of pursuing, intercepting, and destroying
the cruisers of the enemy. This suppression
of attacks upon commerce must no doubt be a

costly operation, though it can hardly be impossible.

At two points the enemy's cruiser can always be found. Its destination is the English merchant ship, and the system of convoys, by which groups of merchant ships are accompanied by armed vessels for their defence, aims at meeting the cruiser at its destination. The second necessary point of his course is furnished by his need to supply himself with coal. He cannot do this at British coaling stations if they are protected by garrisons and such armament as is required to defeat a light attack. He must therefore seek his supplies either at the coaling stations of his own nation, or at neutral ports. There seems no reason except expense to prevent our watching the entrance of every possible coaling port by one of our own cruisers.

It appears to us, in view of the magnitude of the interests at stake, and of the completeness of the protection which would be afforded

by such a policy as has just been described,
that nothing less than this policy ought to be
the object of British naval preparation. We
cannot, however, conceal from ourselves the
fact that our naval force falls at present far
short of that which would be needed for the
adoption of this policy even against a single
maritime rival. The policy recommended
involves in the first place a force of battleships numerous enough to carry out the
blockading or masking system, and in the
second place two very large fleets of cruisers,
the first to act as scouts and messengers for
the combatant fleets, the second to undertake
the duty of patrolling the ocean.

In the policy here described it is important
to distinguish between the substance and the
form. The purpose is to disarm the enemy at
sea, and with this view as soon as possible to
destroy his naval force. The form which is
adopted, that of blockading the enemy's fleets
in their ports, is chosen because it appears to

offer the surest plan of finding them. It tells off against every known portion of the enemy's navy a superior English force, of which the mission is to find and to follow the detachment of the enemy assigned to it, hunting it down incessantly from the outbreak of hostilities until its defeat or until the cessation of the war. A reserve fleet is provided to deal with any portion of the enemy that may escape its immediate pursuers.

That such an escape is possible, it would be rash to deny, in view of the experience of Nelson, who was twice given the slip by the French fleet in Toulon, which it was his mission to watch. Moreover, in our times, the difficulties of close blockade are increased by the existence of torpedo squadrons in the enemy's ports.

To provide against the risk of escape, there are various kinds of precautions which may be taken. In the first place, it is above all desirable that the British fleets should have a superiority of speed. The one thing indispensable for the fleet that seeks to attack is the power of compelling an enemy to fight, just as the one thing desirable for the inferior fleet is the power of avoiding an engagement. In the days of sailing vessels this advantage was sought from what was known as the weather-gage; that is, in a position as directly as might be to windward of the enemy. This was an advantage to be obtained by skilful manœuvring. Under the conditions of steam navigation the direction of the wind has lost most of its importance, and the power to refuse, to accept, or to compel battle rests with the fleet that has the superior speed. The speed of a fleet, however, is measured not by its fastest but its slowest vessel, and it is therefore an object of the greatest importance in the construction of a navy to secure for all the ships built a uniform high speed.

It is possible, however, that under any

circumstances the enemy's detachment may go to sea unobserved. The object of the British admiral would then be to ascertain as soon as possible the direction of its movements. For this purpose the telegraph may render services undreamed of in the days of Nelson. But if the telegraph in war is to render valuable assistance with regard to an enemy's movements, and to be employed for the purpose of assisting the combinations of the British commander-in-chief, it must not be at the mercy of possible enemies or even of possibly unfriendly neutrals.

There appears to be no cable communicating directly between Great Britain and any point south of the line from British Guiana to Cape St. Vincent. Even the cables to Gibraltar touch the land at Lisbon. Nothing would be easier in time of war than to cut off telegraphic communication between England and the South Atlantic, including all the west coast of Africa.

Again, all our telegraphic communication with the East, except that which depends upon Russia, passes either through Egypt or through the district of Asia between Diarbekr and Erzeroum. It is evident, therefore, that our telegraphic communications would in time of war be precarious. But their interruption would be an embarrassment of the gravest nature.

We consider that it is imperatively required for the safety of the Empire, in order to assure in time of war the communication between its various portions, that they should be connected by a series of purely British cables having no shore-ends upon foreign territory. In time of war the admirals would have to lay cables to islands seized by them near the enemy's blockaded ports.

An enemy's fleet which had escaped might conceivably attempt the capture of some British secondary naval base or coaling station. The attempt is not probable, for it would divert the force which undertook it from their objective. If the telegraph service had been properly organised in peace, the English Admiralty would be promptly informed of the enemy's appearance. A very few days would elapse before the arrival of a relieving naval force. Against such a hurried attack, however, the more important coaling stations should be placed in a position of defence. The telegraph is, in our judgment, even more important than the fortifications, for it would greatly facilitate the discovery and consequent defeat of a hostile naval force, which would more than compensate for temporary loss at any exposed station.

A further requirement, of which the urgency is brought into relief by the consideration of the blockading or masking policy, is that of rapid mobilisation. The whole plan falls to the ground unless the masking fleets can be at their posts before the enemy has had time to complete his preparations and put to sea.

This consideration greatly affects our position in the Mediterranean. In the event of a single-handed war between ourselves and the French, for example, the British Mediterranean fleet, as matters stand, would be outnumbered by the French evolutions-squadron, strengthened by its first-class reserve, and might have to fight a decisive battle before it could be reinforced.

With regard to the mode of operations we are now considering, it should be observed that in the calculation of the British force required no account can be taken of that portion of the British Navy which is ordinarily employed upon foreign stations other than the Mediterranean. These vessels could not be concentrated in European waters in time to take part at the beginning of the war in the masking operations, and, moreover, if during peace their presence on their stations is necessary, it can hardly be doubted that it would be still more necessary in war. It is even possible that the outbreak of war might make additional calls upon their activity.

If any reinforcement of the British detachments in distant waters is contemplated by way of preparation for war, the ships required for the purpose must be provided as something additional to the main naval force concentrated against the enemy's principal fleets in his ports.

In attempting to put together this account of the work which the Navy will be called upon to perform in war, we have had a definite practical purpose in view—to ascertain, if possible, the minimum necessary strength at which the British Navy should be maintained. We have started no theory of our own, but have endeavoured to glean from the study of the writings of those strategists, and those naval officers, English and foreign, who have dealt with this question, what are the necessary conditions of a maritime conflict.

Before proceeding to examine what force is

needed to execute the plan we have explained, it may be well to refer to some apparent objections to the plan itself. It has been alleged that an alternative plan exists—the plan which was adopted by one of Lord St. Vincent's predecessors, Lord Howe, of concentrating his main fleet in Torbay with a reserve fleet at St. Helens.

We are unable, however, to find that this policy has any serious advocates, and it is open to the grave objection that it leaves the enemy's fleet free to proceed to any part of the ocean, to support his cruisers, or to make raids upon our own coasts, such as those which have been illustrated by the naval manœuvres of recent years. No doubt Great Britain, if this policy were adopted, would still retain the command of the sea, in the sense that the enemy could not safely undertake the transport of troops for territorial attack; but this plan would leave our sea-borne trade exposed to attack of a character far more serious than any that is possible if the blockading or masking policy be adopted, and would expose the communications between the various ports of the Empire to the enemy's attack until such time as our admirals had solved the exceedingly difficult problem of finding and of forcing to fight an enemy's fleet which had for its first object to avoid a decisive encounter.

The method known as Lord St. Vincent's has in its favour almost all the strategical authorities. It is the policy propounded in the concluding section of the report of the Committee on the Naval Manœuvres of 1888, the admirals laying down " that the Channel fleet should, supposing the enemy to be a great maritime Power, be of sufficient force to blockade the fleets of such Power in their ports, or to bring them to immediate action should they put to sea, and that there should always be an effective reserve squadron." Captain Mahan considers it the only wise policy, and, what is of great importance, is of opinion that any other policy would require, to be effective, a still larger numerical force, and would tend to prolong the struggle.*

We need hardly discuss the objection raised by some military officers at the United Service Institution in 1888, that the adoption of Lord St. Vincent's policy " would logically lead to a reduction of the Army, to the abolition of the Militia, and to sending the Volunteers to inglorious ease in their homes." It appears to us that the only question is, whether the policy is sound. If, being sound, it should lead to the reduction described, so much the better for the tax-payer, though the country is never likely, to use the popular phrase, to " put all its eggs into one basket." The real question is, whether the policy is practicable— in other words, whether blockade in the sense here described, for which we prefer the term

* 'The Influence of Sea Power upon History,' pp. 534, 535.

" masking," is still practicable since the intro-
duction of steam. Happily, however, there is
little doubt upon this point, provided always
that the force employed be sufficient.

The report of the Committee on the Naval
Manœuvres of 1888 authoritatively defines
the proportion of force required. The three
admirals were of opinion that for an efficient
" blockade," the blockading battleships should
be in the proportion of at least five to three
to the enemy's vessels in harbour, while the
proportion of fast cruisers employed in blockading should not be less than two to one of
the blockaded. We thus have the necessary
data for the proper method of comparison
between the British and any other Navy.

It is, of course, of no use whatever, if we
wish to know whether the English Navy is
in a position to perform its defensive function
in a war, say against France, to compare
statistical tables of the numbers of French and
English ironclads and cruisers. The com-

parison, to be of any value, must be based upon the work to be done. We have seen that the principal work consists in masking, if possible, in its ports the enemy's whole navy.

We say advisedly the enemy's "whole navy," because it is obvious that the moment a government holds a war with Great Britain to be probable, its first measure will be to concentrate near home the whole of its avail- able naval force. The enemy's colonies, no doubt, would be in this way left exposed, but if naval victory were secured, the colonies would eventually be saved. Unless it were secured they could not be preserved.

Accordingly, in calculating the minimum necessary strength of the British Navy, we must set down, as the first item, a number of battleships of high uniform speed, exceed- ing in the proportion of five to three those which the probable enemy possess, and of cruisers exactly double the number of the probable enemy's cruisers. These two categories form the necessary masking force.

Secondly, there must be a reserve fleet consisting of line-of-battle ships and cruisers. The report of the admirals lays down that this reserve should be sufficient to hold the Channel, and protect the coast and commerce of the United Kingdom. This is hardly a satisfactory definition, as it gives no indication of what force would be sufficient for the purpose described. It appears to us to rest upon a confusion of thought, for so long as the masking operations are effective, no attack upon our coast is practicable.

Lord St. Vincent's reserve in the Downs comprised six sail of the line and four frigates, while four sail of the line and eight frigates were stationed at various points on the coasts. Considering the numerical diminution of fleets since the time of sailing ships, these figures might perhaps be taken as an indication of the necessary force to be held in reserve.

In addition to the masking and reserve forces, provision must be made for the various foreign stations. For this purpose it is probably not so much an increase of numbers as an increase of efficiency that is required. The practice of employing in distant waters ships of old type, of low speed, and of small armament, is hardly consistent with the fact that these vessels on the outbreak of war cannot be relieved, and may be required to remain on their stations until the conclusion of peace.

Lastly, provision must be made for a sufficient number of cruisers to protect our traders at sea, and whatever method be employed for this purpose, it is evident that safety in this department lies in a liberal estimate of the probable requirements.

The Navy, in spite of the building programme undertaken in 1889, is still far short of the standard laid down by the admirals, certainly in ironclads, and, probably, also in cruisers and torpedo vessels. The number of men is also insufficient for war, and a serious doubt exists as to the value of most if not all of the armour-piercing guns in the possession of the Navy. The first and most crying need of Imperial defence is, therefore, for the construction of new ships, for the increase of the *personnel* of the Navy, and for a searching trial, and if need be, a complete renewal, of the existing naval ordnance.

In December 1888, Lord Charles Beresford, in the House of Commons, examined the British Navy as regards sufficiency for the tasks before it in a possible war with France. He took the principle, to which any plan of campaign must adhere, of watching and endeavouring to destroy every war vessel of the supposed enemy. As the basis of his calculations, he took the return which had been laid before Parliament of the fleets of England, France, and other Powers, and drew up a plan of campaign in which all the English

vessels built and building were accounted
for.

Excluding vessels officially declared unserviceable, the French had 26 battleships, of
which one stationed abroad in distant seas,
and one (Brennus), building, were left out of his
reckoning, while 6 coast-defence vessels were
included, so that there were 30 battleships to
account for. The return of English battleships showed 49, less 8 unserviceable. Of
the 41 others, 5 were in distant seas, leaving
36 to work with.

The distribution of the French Fleet, assumed by Lord Charles Beresford, is shown
in the following table, A. His distribution
of 36 British ships and all the cruisers of
15 knots and over is shown in B.

Both nations have laid down new ships
since 1888, so that 10 more battleships in
England and 7 more in France (beside
the Brennus) will be available when all
now building are completed. Great Britain

	Mediterranean.	Cherbourg.	Brest.	Reserve.	Cruisers to protect Trade.
A. Hypothetical distribution of 30 French battleships of 1888.	15	9 {5 Squadron, 4 Coast defence	6 {4 Squadron, 2 Coast defence		10
B. Hypothetical counter-distribution of British battleships and cruisers of 1888 to watch above (less 33 cruisers of less than 15 knots, not practically useful).	Battleships. 15 / Cruisers. 23	Battleships. 12 / Cruisers. 16	Battleships. 9 / Cruisers. 12		
C. French battleships, when all now building are completed.	Battleships. 18	Battleships. 8	Battleships. 12		
D. English battleships, when all now building are completed.	20	11	·5		
E. Required by admirals to meet C.	30	13	20	3	

will also have 42 cruisers more than in
1888.

The present position is therefore that 46
English battleships are available against 38
French ones. According to the standard of
five to three laid down by our admirals, Great
Britain should have against 38 French battleships 63 battleships, without counting the
reserve squadron. If the reserve is put at the
low figure of 3 battleships, the Navy will be
20 battleships below the standard, when all
the ships now building are complete, even
supposing that in the meantime the French
lay down no more battleships. A hypothetical
distribution of the French Fleet, and of the
English squadrons to watch it, is given in
Tables C and D.

The plan of adding the new ships to those
available in 1888 is not altogether satisfactory,
partly because we complete our vessels more
rapidly than do the French. But if we take
the latest authoritative comparison of the

battleships, that of M. Cochéry, the reporter
to the French Committee on the Estimates, we
find him calculating that in 1892, the French
Navy will have 30 ironclads to Great Britain's
31, in commission and first-class reserve. He
also states that in 1892, the French Navy will
have 40,620 men at sea and in barracks ; but
it should be noted that in the event of war,
they can mobilise any number from the *in-
scription maritime.*

For the defence of those ports outside Great
Britain,. which form secondary bases for the
Navy, something has been done·of late years.
The necessary forts have in most places been
built, and in some cases armed. It is desirable
to insure their communications with Great
Britain, as far as possible by direct telegraph
cables, to complete and maintain their stores
of ammunition and, where necessary, of provisions, and, above all, to provide them permanently with full garrisons. To delay until
the outbreak of war the completion of the

garrisons would be to offer them as prizes to an energetic enemy. The principle of employing local forces for these garrisons wherever trustworthy local troops can be raised is undoubtedly sound. Where there is a difficulty in maintaining a local force, or where its efficiency is doubtful, the garrison must be provided out of Imperial resources.

CHAPTER III.

THE PEACE OF INDIA.

A FRENCH statesman has described in terms that should be familiar to Englishmen the mission of Great Britain in the East, and the difficulty which confronts us there. "The enterprise which the English have undertaken in India deserves the good wishes of all friends of civilisation. To conduct the political and moral education of two hundred and fifty millions of our fellow-creatures is a prodigious task which, nobly begun with this century, will require for its entire fulfilment a succession of efforts continued over a period of time of which the duration cannot be measured in advance. But while we admire the undertaking, we cannot avoid an apprehension which recent events accumulating from day to day more and more prove to be well founded. Will England be able to finish her work? Will peace, the indispensable condition of its completion, be allowed her for the necessary length of time? Will not a neighbour come to interrupt and hinder the execution of her magnanimous designs? Will not another Power try to replace the British Government, at the risk of failing where Great Britain's success gains the sincere approval of all enlightened and impartial minds?"* It would be impossible better to sketch than in these few sentences the two parts of England's mission in regard to India. We have undertaken the political and moral education of the peoples which inhabit that peninsula, and we have therefore implicitly assumed the duty of guarding our

---

* 'L'Inde Anglaise, son état actuel, son avenir,' par T. Barthélemy St.-Hilaire, Membre de l'Institut, Sénateur.   Paris, 1887, p. 1.

work against interruption. We have made ourselves responsible not merely for the Government, but also for the peace of India.

We have there as neighbours two Powers, China and Russia, each of which is in some respect our rival in the Old World. The internal condition of China is such that generations may pass before India is threatened by an aggressive policy on the part of the Celestial Empire. Far different is the case of Russia. We do not assume on the part of the Tsar or his advisers any malignant purpose. But that it is possible for the Russians to wish to replace the English in India, that it is probable that they may attempt to extend their possessions into Afghanistan, and to use their position on the Indian frontier as a lever for exerting influence on our policy in Europe, is self-evident. The rapid advance of Russia in the last few years from the Caspian to Penjdeh can have no other meaning. That there is a point at which Great Britain must

H

oppose Russian advance, should it continue, is
equally clear.   Our object is to ascertain if we
can where this point lies, to examine what
would be the conditions of a possible conflict,
and to what extent the preparations already
made by Great Britain are sufficient to secure
in case of need the object ·desired—the peace
of India.

There are some who think that Russia is
advancing within striking distance of India
only because we thwart her European policy.
We do not in Europe take isolated action
against Russia in matters of European concern,
and we ought not to interfere with her
designs in any case where interference is not
plainly demanded by our interest or our
national honour.   But even if those of whom
we speak are right, precautions are yet needed,
and Indian defence must still be studied.

There are others who, while they admit
that Russia might wish to reach India, deny
her ability to do it, and would " trust to

the Himalayas and the deserts." Unfortunately, our enquiries show us that the enterprise is in itself an undertaking which may
easily become practicable.

In discussing Indian defence, the first point
to settle is the character of the British tenure
of India. It is usual to speak of India as a
conquered country. The phrase is inaccurate
in both its terms. India is not a country, and
the English have not conquered it. It is a
continent of many lands and many races,
differing more widely in soil and climate, in
race, language, and institutions, than do the
countries and peoples of all Europe. The
process by which British rule has established
itself has not been, except in a few isolated
cases, that of breaking the will and overcoming
the resistance of the native populations, to
which the word "conquest" would properly
apply. On the contrary, the East India
Company, originally a trading corporation
enjoying a monopoly, enlisted in its service

(in the first instance to resist the attacks of the French) a body of Indian soldiers. At that time the various dynasties which were preying upon the native races had lost whatever administrative energy they had once possessed, and the general anarchy was such as almost to compel the Company to undertake, in the neighbourhood of its own settlements, the restoration of order. In the end the Company became the paramount power. Its agents were hardly more alien in language, race, and religion from the peoples governed than had been the despots whom they superseded, and its military forces were principally composed of Indian troops. The substitution of Queen Victoria for the Company has changed none of these conditions. Its chief effect has been to introduce into the administration of India a more direct responsibility to the public opinion of Great Britain.

There is in India no Indian nation, and the influence of Western ideas, which we call civilisation, has permeated only the mere surface at a few points of contact. Moslem and Hindoo; Parsee, Pathan and Sikh, are as distinct as ever. It is the innumerable contrasts among the natives themselves that makes a British administration possible.

The defence of a bundle of countries like India is evidently something quite different from that of a country like France, which is in comparison but a small corner of land, and which is inhabited by a united nation. An invader in France is confronted by the determined will of the whole population. Every peasant is an active enemy. To the average Indian peasant a state of things in which his governors should be of the same blood or of the same language with himself is probably inconceivable. That there should be any connection between his own efforts and the destiny of the district in which he lives has hardly occurred to him.

The supremacy of the English rests only

to a limited extent upon their own superior
force.   It is made possible by the divisions
among the natives.   To a great extent our
ascendancy is "moral," resting, that is, upon
character and self-confidence.   To this confidence the natives bow.   It has produced in
them a corresponding belief in the omnipotence
of Great Britain.   For a century the Englishman has behaved in India as a demi-god.   He
accounts himself a superior being, equal in all
the works of war and government to hundreds
of Indians, and the majority of the inhabitants
take him at his own valuation.

Any weakening of this confidence in the
minds of the English or of the Indians would
be dangerous, and it seems certain that this is
one of the difficulties of the present situation.
The report has gone forth in India that there
is another race, the Russian, which faces
British audacity with an audacity of its own.
If this be true, the English are not the
only demi-gods, and for the Indian the test

of its truth is rather the behaviour of the British whom he can observe than of the Russians whom he cannot. If he sees that his Englishmen are uneasy, he may interpret it as a sign of their coming doom. He will wait until their time is up, when he will accept new and stronger masters, and perhaps hasten to put himself on the side of the coming race.

Considerations such as these must needs have weight in determining the policy of the Indian Government. It is evidently undesirable to show signs of weakness in dealing with Russia. The Penjdeh incident, opening as it did the prospect of a possible conflict, is said to have raised in the Indian mind the momentous question. The settlement of 1888 postponed the answer. The Boundary Commission was understood to have traced a line beyond which Russia was not to advance.

The arrangement carries with it far-reaching consequences. If Russia should attempt a

further advance, will it be possible for Great
Britain to allow it without weakening that
moral ascendancy which is so important in
India? The native argument will be that
Russia can have no motive for the attempt
except to drive back the British, and that
they would never let themselves be driven
back unless they were afraid of Russia. What
answer can be given to this argument? What
motive, except a prudence closely akin to fear,
could induce a British Government to acquiesce in a Russian advance?

It is clear that the very nature of the task
which has been undertaken in India imposes
upon the statesman charged with its defence
one condition which can never be violated with
impunity. His policy must avoid the appearance of weakness. It must not shift or change,
it must not promise and fail to perform, it
must not trim to circumstances; but it must
control circumstances in the pursuit of an aim
never lost sight of. The aim is peace in India,

and unbroken confidence in England's mission. Confidence is sure to be shaken by drawing back from a position once adopted. If peace is to be undisturbed in India, it is desirable that war, if war ever becomes necessary, should be as far removed from her borders as possible.

In the event of war with Russia, where is the struggle to take place? In a case like this the theatre of war is not necessarily the district in dispute. Each side seeks to reach the other in that quarter where a blow will be most decisive. The best way to compel England to give up India would be to conquer the British Islands, and the best way to force Russia to abandon her designs in the East would be to take Petersburg and Moscow. Of course, neither of these things is practicable.

The most effective direction actually open for a Russian attack upon the British Empire is that which leads from Central Asia to

India. A secondary operation would be the
interruption of communication between India
and the rest of the Empire. This could
be carried out effectively only in case Russia
obtained the co-operation of a maritime power
of the first rank. Russia herself could not at
present touch these communications, and even
the Suez route would be perfectly safe as
long as the British fleet is undefeated in the
Mediterranean. The temporary obstruction of
the Suez Canal would not prevent the use of
the Isthmus.

In regard to the vulnerability of Russia by
Great Britain, a number of suggestions have
been made which we enumerate for the purpose of pointing out the reasons which appear
to us to make them impracticable.

Some damage might be inflicted upon
Russia by the close blockade of her ports,
but her land frontiers are so extensive, and
her maritime resources so slightly developed,
that the pressure thus exercised would amount

not to distress, but merely to inconvenience. It would certainly not suffice to bring about the abandonment of her design.

The pet project of one school is to attack Russia with an expeditionary force landed at some points on the coast of the Black Sea. No doubt if Great Britain could land in southern Russia an army strong enough to defeat the armies of European Russia, and to march to Moscow, this would be decisive. But, short of this, an attack upon Russia in Europe would hardly serve the purpose. The Russian army in Europe counts, on a peace-footing, over 700,000 combatants, while its war strength exceeds two millions, without counting non-combatants. To attack these masses with even 100,000 British troops would scarcely be prudent.

Another proposal is to land an expeditionary force at a point to the south of the Caucasus, and to march through Tiflis towards the Caspian. The Russian army of the Caucasus numbers 100,000 men on a peace-footing, and double that number on mobilisation. The distance between the Black Sea and the Caspian (about 450 miles) is longer than that which separates the British frontier in India from Russian Turkestan.

Suppose the Russian force defeated, and the English at the Caspian, it would still be necessary to defeat the Russians on the Caspian Sea itself, before their communications towards India would be interrupted. Before this could be effected a decisive battle must have been fought on the Indian frontier. If it were a Russian victory, the operations on the Caspian might fail to save India. If it were a defeat, they would have been unnecessary. The Russians, moreover, can always reinforce their army in the Caucasus long before any British force could reach Tiflis, so that the success of the expedition is very problematical. No doubt, its advocates contemplate the co-operation of the Turkish

army ; but the Turks have never been able
during the present century to conduct offensive operations, and the Russian frontier in
Armenia is guarded by fortresses which the
Turks will certainly never retake. It may be
doubted whether a trustworthy alliance with
Turkey could be obtained when the object
was the defence, not of Turkey, but of India,
and, without such an alliance and the assured
friendship of France, the British forces in the
Black Sea might find themselves caught in a
trap from which there would be no escape.
Moreover, in the event of war with the United
Kingdom, Russia might perhaps contrive to
seal the entrance to the Black Sea, either at
the Bosphorus or at the Dardanelles.

Still more impracticable are the proposals
to land an expeditionary force at the Gulf of
Iskanderoon, near Cyprus, or in the Persian
Gulf. The Russian outposts in Armenia are
over 300 miles from Iskanderoon, while the
Transcaspian railway is more than 700 miles

distant from the Persian Gulf or the Indian
Ocean.   There is no railway and no good road
available from either of these proposed sea
bases.   The districts to be traversed are difficult, and afford no sufficient supplies.   It
would be simply impossible, operating on
either of these lines, to move a force into
a position from which it could menace the
Russian communications.

At Vladivostock in the Pacific, Russia is undoubtedly vulnerable.   A British fleet, assisted
by an expeditionary force to be landed, would
be able to invest and in time destroy the
place.   But it may be doubted whether the
blow would be so severe as to compel Russia
to concentrate all her energies to avert it,
and whether she would not better defend or
recover Vladivostock by a resolute attack upon
the Indian frontier.   Tempting, therefore, as
is the plan for destroying Russian authority
on the Pacific, in the event of war, yet, if a
Russian attack on India is feasible, we might

find that we had not checked it by our counter-move.

It thus appears that all the plans that have been mooted for the indirect defence of India by an attack upon Russia's communications or by a counter-attack in Europe or Asia are either impracticable or highly doubtful in themselves. They all have the further disadvantage of dispersing the British forces. The only remaining course, is the direct defence of India upon her own borders.

The specific military task of the British Empire can now be clearly defined. On the north-west border of India the British sphere of influence has become conterminous with that of a great military Power which may at any time become aggressive. It is necessary to be ready to repel the attack if it should be made. The conflict must be fought out in the debateable border-lands. It cannot be transferred to any other theatre of war, because in none would success be assured, or a decisive result be obtained. It cannot be transferred to India without the abandonment of large districts already under British rule, and without the inevitable loss of influence which such a step would entail. To concentrate in time in these border-lands in a suitable position a force sufficient to ensure success must be the prime object of British military administration. All other military ends are subordinate, and consist either in supplements to the action of the Navy, or in provision for the possibility of its failure.

CHAPTER IV.

THE NORTH-WEST FRONTIER.

No judgment concerning the defence of India can be formed without a knowledge of the geography of the region in which operations might take place. Not that geography is the only factor in the problem. Other elements have to be considered, such as the political conditions already touched upon, and the forces available, which remain to be examined hereafter. But without geography neither political nor strategical wisdom can go far.

Unfortunately, in regard to the countries with which Indian defence has to deal, it is impossible to refer to well-known text-books or maps. There are no text-books, and all but

I

the most recent maps are untrustworthy. Accurate knowledge of many of the districts has not been acquired until a date so recent that it is embodied in no atlas, and in no generally accessible map. Our investigation, therefore, cannot proceed except with the aid of a hitherto unwritten chapter of geography. We must either abandon our search or must place before our readers a sketch of the countries between India and the Russian border.

The Indian frontier in this direction is, roughly speaking, a straight line from the north-west corner of Kashmir to the mouth of the Indus, a distance of about 1000 miles. To the east of this line lies India, where England has a mission to fulfil, of which the prime condition is peace. To the west of it lies the region where that peace may be challenged, and where it must be secured.

The first thing to realise is the size of this border-land. It extends from the Oxus on the north to the Arabian Sea on the south, a distance of 800 miles, that is, as far as from

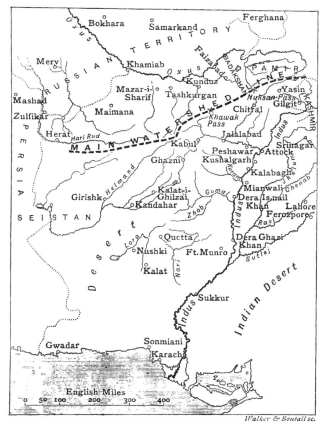

Walker & Boutall sc.

Paris to Dantzig or Buda-Pesth.   From the

Persian frontier between Mashad and Herat to the boundary of Kashmir, is over 700 miles; farther, that is, than from Venice to Copenhagen. The northern edge of Kashmir is 240 miles from Attock, and from Attock a straight line to the mouth of the Indus measures 650 miles. No European country except Russia offers dimensions such as these.

A line drawn from Sukkur on the Indus (500 miles below Attock) to Herat, roughly divides the whole region into two halves, a southern and a north-eastern, which it is convenient to treat separately.

In the southern section mountains run due north from the sea at Karachi to Quetta and the Khwaja Amran. West of these ranges the southern part of the section is a plateau of which the ridges run east and west. The northern part of it is a huge plain desert except upon the banks of the Helmand

The north-eastern section is all mountains.

It does indeed include a narrow plain on the right bank of the Indus, and a somewhat wider plain on the left bank of the Oxus ; but with these small exceptions, the whole space between Indus and Oxus is a mass of tangled mountains, surpassing in every dimension all that merely European experience would enable us to conceive. The mountains of Kashmir are higher than the Pyrenees piled upon the Alps. The ranges which end to the east of Herat, and of which only the lower offshoots protect that city, are what the Pyrenees would be if they were flanked on each side by several other chains of equal mass and elevation. The range that looks down upon the plain of the Indus carries its peaks in the north to the height of Mont Blanc ; in the centre to that of the Maladetta, and even where towards Sukkur it dies away in comparatively trifling hills, the last tiny spur is equal in mass and height to the whole Snowdon range.

*

The principal valley in this mountain region is that of Kabul, an oval basin about the size of Derbyshire, with its longer axis from north to south. The valley bottom is over 5000 ft. above the sea, and the mountain walls are 5000 or 6000 ft. above the plain. This valley is prolonged towards the north-east by that of Panjshir, which runs up to the Hindu Kush at the Khawak Pass. To the south the Kabul valley is connected by several roads over low spurs of the hills with Ghazni, and from Ghazni the valley extends without a break to Kalat-i-Ghilzai and the plain of Kandahar. This long series of valleys, which may be briefly described as the Kabul-Kandahar depression, is the most obvious natural dividing line through the mountains.

A second depression runs from Kabul to Peshawar, following roughly the line of the Kabul river. It is bounded on the south, at a distance of about 30 miles from the river,

by the Safed Koh or White Mountains, which
send their spurs at both ends of the valley up
to and across the river, which has cut through
them in a gorge. In the plain between these
spurs lies Jalálábad, from which roads lead

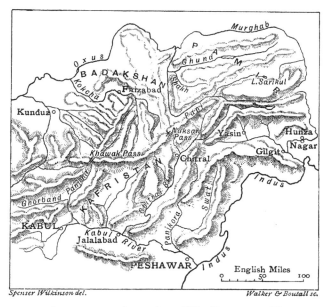

Spenser Wilkinson del.   Walker & Boutall sc.

over the spurs by the Khaibar or Tartara
Passes to Peshawar, and by the Lataband or
the Jagdalak and Haft Passes to Kabul.

Just below Jalálábad, the Kabul river
receives a tributary from the north-east, the
river Chitral. This stream rises only 10
miles south of the head-waters of the Oxus, to
which for 50 miles it runs parallel, separated
only by a single chain of peaks. It then
turns south-westward, and flows for 200 miles
along a deep valley between two spurs of the
Hindu Kush, which accompany it almost to
its junction with the Kabul. To the north of
Jalálábad, between the rivers of Panjshir and
of Chitral, the country known as Kafristan
is unexplored, although it has been visited,
under difficulties, by Dr. Robertson, Mr.
Kitchen, and Mr. McNair, with surveying
parties.

The Chitral river is shut in on the east by
an unbroken wall of mountains, behind which
(to the east) lie in the north the valleys of
Yasin and Gilgit, pouring their waters east-
ward to the Indus, and in the south the
valleys of Panjkora and Swat, which send

their streams southwards to the Kabul river near Peshawar. The whole country between the Indus, the Upper Oxus, and Kafristan is extremely rugged. The peaks, ranging from 18,000 to 25,000 ft., are wrapped in perpetual snow; the valleys are deep and narrow, the passes few and high. There is no fertile area where a considerable town could grow, and no district in which a large force could find food or shelter. There are no cart-roads, and few, if any, roads passable by laden mules.

The water-parting between the Oxus and the river of Chitral has already been mentioned. It is the most northerly chain of the Hindu Kush, and overlooks the Pamir plateau ("the roof of the world"), a square table-land level with the top of Mont Blanc, enclosed by the two streams which, rising at its south-eastern corner, flow, the one along its southern and western sides, the other round its eastern and northern sides, to meet at its north-western

corner and to form the main stream of the
Oxus.

The Hindu Kush follows the southern margin of the Pamir as far as the south-west
corner of the plateau.   Then, at the Nuksan
Pass, the main ridge of the Hindu Kush turns
west-south-west, and continues in this direction
in a straight line for 550 miles, forming the
watershed and the line of the highest peaks,
which are grouped as they proceed westward
under various names, and end with the Koh-i-
Wala, 80 miles south-east of Herat.   The
Nuksan Pass is 16,500 ft. high, and the last
peak of the Koh-i-Wala 11,600.   For 250
miles westward of the Nuksan Pass the watershed line nowhere, even at the passes, falls
below 11,600 ft.

Between the Nuksan and Khawak Passes,
the Hindu Kush is really unknown.   Its
southern spurs fill up Kafristan.   Its northern
spurs jut out nearly 200 miles, forcing the
Oxus to bend away to the north.   The hill

country between the main chain and this bend of the Oxus is Badakshan, with Faizabad for its chief town.

South of the Safed Koh, and between the Indus and the Kabul-Kandahar depression, lies a border-land of the greatest importance. The mountains here have the shape of the figure 5, the horizontal top-stroke being the Safed Koh, and the point at the lower end being the summit of Takatu, 11,000 ft. high, near Quetta. The short perpendicular line represents a row of peaks from 14,000 ft. high in the north to 13,000 in the south. The curve may be divided into two halves, meeting at Fort Munro, where the hills approach nearest to the Indus (at Dera Ghazi Khan). In the middle of the northern half rise the peaks of Solomon's Throne (Takht-i-Suliman), 11,000 ft. high, opposite Dera Ismail Khan on the Indus, and north of them, nearer to the corner, the still higher peaks of Kanigurum. Between Fort Munro and Takatu no peaks reach 8000 ft., but many ranges here run

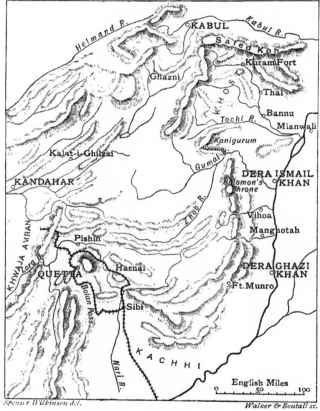

Spenser Wilkinson del.   *Walker & Boutall sc.*

parallel, following the general line of the curve.

The rivers of this figure 5 require special attention. In the corner where the horizontal and perpendicular lines meet (between the Peiwar and Shutargardan Passes), rises the Kuram, which flows south-eastward (parallel to the curve) to the Indus opposite Mianwali. On the Kuram lie Kuram Fort, Thal, and Bannu, above which town it is joined by the river of Khost, a valley in the corner where the perpendicular line meets the curve.

All the other rivers rise west of the moun tains, in the space enclosed by the curve, which is a table-land little higher than the Kabul-Kandahar depression, and is overlooked by the curved rim, which the rivers pierce, form-ing passes named after them. The chief of these streams are the Tochi, rising west of the Kanigurum mountains, winding round their northern base to join the Kuram, close to the Indus, and the Gumal, which passes north of the Takht-i-Suliman to join the Indus below Dera Ismail.

The Gumal is formed by the union of the three chief streams of the highland plateau, one from the north-west, a second from the west, and the third, the most important, called the Zhob, from the south-west. Between the Takht-i-Suliman and Fort Munro the streams which emerge from the hills near Vihoa and Mangrotah form passes called after those towns. The waters of the southern half of the curve flow south-westwards towards Sibi, and join the Nari, which runs due southwards towards the Indus, but dries up before reaching it.

Between the upward curve of the southern Sulimans and the north and south range Karachi-Quetta lies the plain of Kachhi, from which the Harnai and Bolan Passes lead through the meeting of the two ranges to Quetta and the small plain of Pishin. This little plain is separated from the plain of Kandahar (or of the great desert) by the Khwaja Amran range, through which the Lora empties the waters of Pishin into the desert, where they form a swamp.

The Indus at Attock enters a region of hills, through which it passes in a long gorge to Kalabagh, 80 miles to the south. From Kalabagh to the sea it flows through a plain in which its bed is wide and shifting. In the summer freshets its volume of water is eleven times as great as in winter. Thus, during the summer it is a torrent in the gorge and a flood in the plains. In winter it is often so shallow as to be difficult of navigation. Permanent bridges are impracticable, except where the banks are fixed and firm, that is, at Attock, at Kushalgarh (35 miles south of Attock), where however there is no bridge, and at Sukkur. The plain to the east of the Indus is almost entirely desert.

The Kabul-Kandahar depression has its northern end at the Khawak Pass (11,600 ft.) crossing the main watershed. To the west of the Khawak Pass the mountains form a pear-

shaped group 400 miles long and 250 miles
wide, of which the watershed line is the long

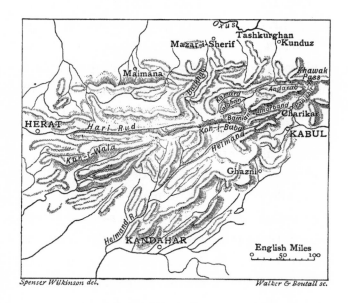

Spenser Wilkinson del.　　　Walker & Boutall sc.

axis, the stalk being at the Khawak Pass, and
the base at the Koh-i-Wala.　One side of the
pear overlooks the Kabul-Kandahar depression,
the other side fronts the plain of the Oxus.
In the narrow part of the pear the peaks

average 15,000 ft. : in its broader part they almost all attain to 11,000 but seldom exceed 12,000 ft.

Formidable as it seems, this mountain tract is not impassable. It is divided in the direction of its long axis by a continuous series of valleys running east and west, and connected by practicable though not easy passes. The Ghorband valley opens at its lower (eastern) end into that of Kabul at Charikar. To the west it is joined by the Shibar Pass to the vale of Bamian. Other passes join the vale of Bamian to that of the Balkh-ab, and this to that of the Hari Rud, the river of Herat. Thus the Herat-Bamian-Ghorband depression runs across the country east and west to meet that of Kandahar and Kabul north of the latter city.

From all these east and west valleys there are roads for horse and foot, but not for carts, leading through or over the mountains to the plain at Kunduz, Tashkurgan (Khulm),

K

Mazar-i-Sharif (Balkh), and Maimana.   Each
of these roads has, however, several ranges
to cross before reaching the plain.

South of the Herat-Bamian valleys and of
the watershed chain the country is unexplored.
Its valleys (inhabited by Hazara tribes) run
towards the south-west, carrying the waters of
the Helmand and its tributaries, which eventually form a lake or marsh in the desert of
Seistan.

There is a direct road from Kabul by the
Unai Pass to the upper Helmand, and thence
either by the Irak Pass to Bamian or along
the south side of the Koh-i-Baba to the valley
of the Hari Rud and Herat.   Along this last-
named route especially, great pains were spent
by the Afghans in 1885 upon the improvement
of the roads.   There is also a road from the
Hazarajat or upper Helmand valley to Ghazni.

The difficulty of all the routes which have
been referred to arises rather from their length
and from their character as defiles than from

their height. One road, the best known, may
be taken as a sample. It is that from Tashkurgan (Khulm) by Bamian to Kabul. Upon
this route there are no less than ten passes, of
which the more important from north to south
are the Kisil (9000 ft.), the Kara (10,500),
leading to the valley of Kamard, the Dendan
Shikan (9000), leading to the valley of Saighan,
the Ak Kobat (11,000), leading to Bamian, the
Great Irak (13,000) over the watershed line,
and the Unai (11,000).

According to Dr. Javorski, who crossed
them all twice, none of these passes is
really difficult, though the Dendan Shikan
and the Kara are "most uncomfortable."
Not one of them is covered with perpetual
snow, and the highest is snow-clad only
from December to March. North of Bamian
there are three places where the road runs
for several miles through a deep chink in
the rocks, between which there is now and
then not enough room for two horsemen to

к 2

pass one another. Under such conditions there can be no wheeled transport. But horse and foot find little difficulty, provided they are unopposed. In the mountains, however, no sustenance can be found, except for small parties.

The roads from Kandahar to Herat skirt the foot of the mountains, and are practicable for wheeled vehicles, as are also those from Kandahar to Kabul, and from Kabul to Peshawar.

The Russian frontier at present runs from Zulficar, on the Hari Rud, 100 miles from Herat, to Khamiab on the Oxus. Thence it follows the line of the Oxus as far as the east of Badakshan, and then runs across the Pamir plateau. The south-western part of the Pamir, comprising the districts of Shignan and Wakhan, is Afghan. The south-eastern portions are Chinese.

A Russian statesman proposing to himself the overthrow of the British power in India, would examine the countries which have now been described with a view to the most effective and the most convenient direction for the advance. We may attempt to follow his analysis.

The routes on the Russian left, leading from the Pamir through Chitral and Gilgit, are so difficult that until recent events it had been the habit to leave them out of consideration. They could never, it was thought, be used for bodies of troops, so long as the Russian frontier was not advanced to the Hindu Kush. The Russians have shewn by their recent action that they attach importance to this region. While it is true that only small bodies can move by these mountain routes, it is equally true that such small bodies are enough to conquer the natives, as our Gilgit force has proved. When a district of this sort has been occupied, it becomes a safe road up to the limit of the occupied area, so that many small bodies may be passed through in succession, and, if there is a suitable place for their collection, an army can thus be pushed on by degrees.

On the Russian right there is the route Penjdeh, Herat, Kandahar, Sukkur. Supposing a Russian army to reach Sukkur, it would still be far from the centres of Indian life. In front would be the Indian desert, and the army, to reap the fruits of its march, would have still either to cross the desert towards Gujerat and Bombay, or to march up the Sutlej to Lahore and Delhi.

From the Russian centre there is the alternative route through Afghan Turkestan and Kabul. The distance from the Oxus east or west of Badakshan by Kabul to Attock is no greater than that from Penjdeh to Kandahar. A Russian army at Attock would be only a few marches from Lahore, and separated by no great natural obstacle from the valleys of the Jumna and the Ganges, which contain the bulk of the population of India.

As regards the effectiveness of the blow, there can be no comparison between the two directions. An army crossing the Indus at Sukkur would be striking the air. An army advancing from Attock would be striking at the heart of India.

On the northern route, once the Indus is crossed, the country is populous, the density of the population increasing with the advance. But between Sukkur and Delhi or Gujerat lies the most sparsely populated region of India. In a populous district, a moving army can almost always find food enough for the short period of its passage, but where there is no population there are no supplies. Accordingly, on the southern route, the army must carry with it or draw from its base supplies to last until Gujerat or Lahore has been reached. But no army can thus supply itself when the length of its march is 1000 miles. The contemplated operation from Penjdeh by Kandahar and Sukkur is therefore out of the question.

From the Oxus opposite to Balkh, Khulm, and Kunduz to the Indus near Attock, the distance is about 400 miles. Wheeled transport is practicable only from the Kabul valley to the Indus. Would it be possible for this distance to be traversed by an army of, say, 50,000 men?

The force would no doubt be subdivided into several columns, to cross by different routes the main watershed range, and to converge at Kabul. Even then the difficulties would be immense. In 1880, Sir Donald Stewart marched a force of 7000 combatants from Kandahar to Kabul, and later in the year Sir Frederick Roberts marched from Kabul to Kandahar with 10,000 combatants. The distance is about 300 miles, and in each case the column was relieved of all superfluous weight. Yet in the first case 6000 and in the second case 8000 transport animals were required. In the operation contemplated, the whole of the supplies would need to be drawn from beyond the Oxus. The Kabul valley would not supply the army for more than a few days, and the many high passes would greatly add to the difficulties. The movement can, therefore, hardly be regarded as practicable.

It appears, then, that the advance of a Russian army from the present frontier, either by Herat and Kandahar, or by Kabul, for the invasion of India, is not a practicable operation. The leap is too great.

Such a leap is, however, hardly consonant with the traditions of Russian policy, which point to a more gradual advance, by easy stages and with long intervals of fresh preparation. The successive stages of this movement are clearly indicated by geographical conditions.

The line from Herat to Bamian, north of the Koh-i-Baba, and thence along the north side of the Hindu Kush, forms a first goal. The distances are nowhere excessive.

The advanced posts have lateral communication with one another, and are covered in their front by the high snow-clad ranges. An occupation of this line for a few years would admit of the preparation of roads behind it, of the accumulation of stores, and of the fortification of important points. The Russians, and their English friends, have continually proposed to us a partition of Afghanistan which would bring them to this line of frontier.

A second advance, to be undertaken perhaps after some years' delay, if we had not entered Kabul at all risks, would lead to the Kabul-Kandahar depression. It might be subdivided by a pause in the Panjshir, Ghorband, and Helmand valleys.

From the Kabul-Kandahar line to the neighbourhood of the Indus would be the third stage.

The advance of the Russian Power to within sight of the Indus would not make the defence of India impossible. But it would render necessary a high state of military preparation and elaborate frontier defences, such as exist, for example, in France and in Germany. This would be an intolerable burden upon Indian finance, and the perpetual danger of serious attack would undermine the confidence in British rule, and sap the foundations of England's work in India. Accordingly, successive governments have refused to admit the hypothesis, and have taken measures to prevent its realisation. Promises of help against Russian attack have been given to the rulers of Kabul, and the position of Quetta has been occupied and fortified and connected by roads and railways with Karachi, and with the line from Ferozpore to Peshawar. The railway has been carried beyond Quetta, through the Khwaja Amran range to the edge of the Kandahar plain.

The object of these measures is to close against a Russian army the roads from Herat to Sukkur, and from Herat by Kandahar to

Kabul. A British force in the Kandahar plain would dispute the Russian advance either way. It could always anticipate the Russians at Kandahar. This value of Quetta depends of course upon the presence there of a force sufficient to form, besides the garrison of the fortress, a strong field army. The Indian forces at present can, with the addition of six battalions from beyond the sea, dispose for this purpose of two army corps (70,000 men), a number equal to any that the Russians from their present frontier could move forwards towards Kandahar.

A Russian advance through Herat is therefore in present conditions impracticable, except to a point short of Kandahar, say to Girishk, where the Herat-Kandahar road crosses the Helmand. Nor can the Russians use the road from Herat through Kandahar to Kabul.

What Russia might undertake from her present frontier is an advance to Herat and Kabul. The natural stages of such a move, which might be taken either all at once, or after successive pauses, are : first to Herat, Maimana, Mazar-i-Sherif, Tashkurgan, Kunduz and Faizabad ; secondly, from this line up to the watershed along its whole length ; and thirdly, from the watershed line to Kabul.

It seems to be generally agreed that the Indian Government cannot safely allow a Russian garrison to enter and hold Kabul, because such a state of things would shake the moral foundations of the British power in India. It is, however, doubtful whether a Russian occupation of Kabul can be prevented if even the first stage of the advance just described has been effected without English counter-action or counter-preparation. The question, to be fairly answered, involves some inquiry into the local political conditions.

The kingdom of Kabul is, properly speaking, confined to a small area—a circle with a radius of 90 miles from the city. Its limits are Jalálábad, the Hindu Kush, the upper Hel-

mand (only 60 miles from Kabul), and Ghazni.*
Within this area, the people are mainly of one
race, language, and religion. The kings of
Kabul, supported by this population, have been
able to assert a suzerainty over the districts
of Kandahar, Herat, and the Oxus valley or
Afghan Turkestan. But their authority, except at Kandahar, has always been precarious, resting upon garrisons of their own
troops.

The district of Kandahar is inhabited by

* The limit of Afghanistan proper is the snow-line
of the Hindu Kush and the Koh-i-Baba. But between
the two ranges is a break, which allows of two roads
(the Irak and Shibar Passes) into Bamian, to which
valley access from the north is by no means easy.
Accordingly, a strong Afghan ruler opposed to a weak
ruler at Kunduz and Mazar-i-Sharif has usually
asserted authority in Bamian, and sometimes in
Saighan and Kámard. In 1840 the farthest point
occupied by British forces was Bájgah, in Kámard.
Bamian, Saighan, and Kámard are all accessible from
east and west. It seems probable, therefore, that the
Russians, once in Afghan Turkestan, would turn and
secure Kámard, Saighan, and Bamian, and that their
outposts would reach to the Irak and Shibar Passes.

Duranis, and between Kalat-i-Ghilzai and Kabul are spread Ghilzai tribes, both Duranis and Ghilzais being akin to the Yusufzais of the Kabul region. Tribes akin to the Yusufzais, Duranis, and Ghilzais, and known in general as Pathans, inhabit the whole country between the Kabul-Kandahar line and the Indus. They are independent clans, with no overlord, living in perpetual feud with one another. The basin of the Helmand, so far as it lies in the mountains, is inhabited by Hazaras, a Mongol race who mix little with the Afghans, and of whom and of whose country little is known. North of Herat live tribes who are as much Turkoman as Afghan, and the whole country north of the watershed is Afghan by government and by garrison rather than by race.

Eastern Baluchistan from the Bolan Pass southwards is inhabited by tribes resembling the Pathans, whose overlord in past times was the Khan of Kalat. The Baluchis for many years have acknowledged the suzerainty of the Government of India.

The whole country north of the Baluch desert and of the Bolan line may be said to fall politically into three groups : the Pathan tribes ; the kingdom of Kabul with Kandahar (Afghanistan proper) ; and the dependencies of the kingdom, that is, the Hazaras of the hills, the district of Herat, and Afghan Turkestan.

The dependencies can be expected to make no resistance of their own to conquest or annexation. If the Afghan garrisons were expelled, and Russian or English garrisons took their place, the populations here would acquiesce in the change so long as the new rule was not more oppressive than the old one.

Among the Pathans each clan has its chief, whose rule is limited by the assembly of headmen. Sometimes a group of clans has a higher chief, who among the independent clans is elected. The British Government, by judicious dealing with the chiefs and councils, and the occasional use of force, has in recent years acquired a paramount influence over the tribes not merely of the Bolan and Harnai Passes, but of all the districts between the Indus, Pishin, and the Zhob or southern affluent of the Gumal river. It is probable that by the ǀadoption of the same policy British influence could without great difficulty be extended right up to the watershed of the Indus, throughout the whole region south of the Safed Koh.

There is a current belief, amounting almost to a superstition, that Afghanistan proper is an especially invincible region, owing partly to its mountainous surroundings and partly to a love of independence peculiar to the Afghans, who are thought of as blood-thirsty, cruel, and treacherous beyond or-dinary mortals.

An impartial examination of the evidence bears out none of these opinions. The

L

Afghans no doubt have the insensibility to
the sufferings of their enemies that is common to their Mohammedan neighbours, and
perhaps to all Eastern races. Their views
of the extent to which deceit is admissible
in war are those of Murat rather than of
Wellington. But they are manly, hospitable,
and courteous. Mr. Charles Masson lived in
Kabul as a visitor for several years prior to the
diplomatic mission of the infatuated Burnes,
who brought about the first Afghan war. Mr.
Masson's account of the people is therefore of
the greatest value, for no other European has
ever had the same intimate acquaintance with
them. "There are few places," he wrote,
"where a stranger so soon feels himself at
home and becomes familiar with all classes as
at Kabul. There can be none where all classes
so much respect his claim to civility and so
much exert themselves to promote his satisfac-
tion and amusement." No doubt it has been
difficult since 1839 for an Englishman to

follow Mr. Masson's example, and to live at Kabul unmolested.

In 1838–9 the Indian Government sent an army to invade the country and to set up an unpopular king, whom Macnaghten and Burnes made ridiculous. The garrison left at Kabul was too weak to overcome resistance, was itself attacked and besieged, and its commanders committed the incredible folly of negotiating for their retreat. The Afghans, as was to be expected, negotiated only to get the force into their power, and destroyed it before it could reach Jalálábad. But they took care of the ladies and officers who were their prisoners, who suffered no unreasonable hardships. Before the conduct of the Afghans can be held to prove them specially treacherous or bloodthirsty, it ought to be settled whether the previous conduct of the English did not afford them some justification.

The bravery of the Afghans is admitted, yet four times the country has been invaded and temporarily held by very small forces. The invading army of 1838–9 numbered 14,500 men, of whom hardly more than half entered the Kabul district. The force destroyed in the passes numbered about 3000, of whom 500 were Europeans. The second invasion, of 1842, was executed with 8000 men from Jalálábad, and about 3000 from Kandahar. The force which in 1879 marched from the Kuram valley to Kabul, and maintained itself there during the winter and spring against the most strenuous efforts of the Afghans, hardly amounted to 8000 men, of whom only a portion were Europeans. It is true that during the war of 1879–80 as many as 55,000 men (16,000 Europeans) were employed. But the greater part of them were engaged in the defence of the Khyber, Kuram, and Bolan routes through the lands of the frontier Pathans.

The difficulty and expense of conquering and holding Kabul was due to the fact that the base was in 1839–42 at Ferozpore, 450 miles, and in 1878–80 at Peshawar, 150 miles from Kabul, so that in both cases a long line of communications had to be protected against hostile attacks.

An invasion and occupation from a base on the borders of the Kabul district would be a much simpler task. Such a base would exist if the English with railways behind them were at Jalálábad, at Kuram, and at the western end of the Gumal Pass. An even nearer base would be furnished to the Russians by the occupation of Bamian and the Anderab valley, both north of the great watershed. The experience of former wars seems to prove that from either of these bases 10,000 men could successfully invade Kabul, though to maintain themselves, if resistance continued, they would require reinforcement.

The Afghan resistance alone can thus in no case be a really serious obstacle to either of the two great Powers if either of them were bent on the conquest of the country. In Herat and Afghan Turkestan, a single decisive defeat of the Afghan army would settle the matter. In the Kabul region there would probably be a vigorous rising after the annexation; but a Power determined to hold the country would crush this rising so relentlessly that it would never be repeated.

The Afghans would, perhaps, resist a Russian attack upon Afghan Turkestan. They would certainly not unaided be successful in their resistance, and possibly, if the attack were undertaken with a strong force, would prefer to make terms.

Provided the attack be unprovoked, they have the promise of English help.

The first promise was made by Lord North-brook to Shere Ali in 1873. In case of attack upon his dominions the Amir was to refer to the Indian Government, which would en-deavour by negotiation to avert hostilities. If unable to succeed in this, India would afford the Amir assistance in the shape of arms and money, and, in case of necessity, would also send troops. The British Government was to be the judge of the occasion, nature, and extent of such assistance. Shere Ali was dissatisfied with this promise, and he objected to receive British agents into his dominions. When the reception of agents was pressed upon him, he refused it, strengthened, no doubt, by promises of Russian help, and the war of 1879–80 was the consequence.

The present Amir Abdurrahman, before he was recognised by the Indian Government, made a very frank statement of his position. He explained his desire " that as long as your Empire and that of Russia exist, my countrymen the tribes of Afghanistan should live quietly in ease and peace ; that these two states should find us true and faithful, and that we should rest at peace between them ; for my tribesmen are unable to struggle with empires, and are ruined by want of commerce ;

and we hope of your friendship that sympathising with and assisting the people of Afghanistan, you will place them under the honourable protection of the two Powers." *

The Amir was then informed, on behalf of the British Government, that, "With regard to the position of the ruler of Kabul to foreign Powers, since the British Government admit no right of interference by foreign Powers in Afghanistan, and since both Russia and Persia are pledged to abstain from all political interference with Afghanistan affairs, it is plain that the Kabul ruler can have no political relations with any foreign Power except the English ; and if any such foreign Power should attempt to interfere in Afghanistan, and if such interference should lead to unprovoked aggression on the Kabul ruler, then the British Government will be prepared to aid him, if necessary, to repel it, provided that he follows the advice of the British Government in regard

* Blue Book, Afghanistan (1881), No. 1, p. 46.

to his external relations." * The Amir thereupon wrote : " About my friendly relations
and communications with foreign Powers, you
have written that I should not have any without advice and consultation with you. You
should consider well that if I have the friendship of a great government like yours, how can
I communicate with another Power without
advice from and consultation with you. I
agree to this. . . .

" You have kindly written that should any
unwarranted attack be made by any other
Power on Afghanistan, you will under all circumstances afford me assistance ; and you will
not permit any other person to take possession
of the territory of Afghanistan. This also is
my desire, which you have kindly granted." †

This letter was acknowledged in the following terms : " I am directed to inform you that
the Government of India are rejoiced that

* Afghanistan (1881), No. 1, p. 47.
† *Ib.* p. 48.

the friendly explanations which have been furnished to you have fulfilled your wishes, and that you appreciate the objects of the Government." *

Sir Lepel Griffin, who in 1880 conducted these negotiations, wrote in 1889: "The letters which I gave to the Amir on the part of the Viceroy are still in force, and regulate his position, and further engage us absolutely to defend him against Russian attack on condition of his following our advice and directions in his foreign policy." †

The promises made in 1880 to the Amir Abdurrahman have since been confirmed, both by words and by actions.

In 1885 the Amir came to India, and Lord Dufferin of course asked for instructions what he should say. After this the Viceroy publicly declared at Rawal Pindi, that so long as the

* Mr. (now Sir) Lepel Griffin to Sirdar Abdul Rahman Khan, July 2, 1880.—Afghanistan (1881), No. 1, p. 49.

† *Asiatic Quarterly Review*, July, 1889, p. 221.

Amir conformed to our advice his enemies would be ours. The Amir in his reply left out the limitation, and Lord Dufferin took no exception to the terms in which the Afghan ruler stated the alliance—terms which were very strong.

Between 1885 and 1888 the frontier of Afghanistan, from the Hari Rud to the Oxus has been delimited by agreement with Russia. In these negotiations Great Britain acted throughout in behalf of the Amir, so that British control of the foreign relations of Afghanistan has been solemnly recognised both by the Tsar and by the Amir.*

* In our account of the negotiations of 1880 the words actually used to and by the Amir have been given. The effect of the notes exchanged is not modified by the fact that in the actual negotiations the Government was committed further than was intended. Lord Hartington's despatch of May 21, 1880, says : " Her Majesty's Government are prepared to renew the assurances which were offered in 1873 by Lord North- brook to the Amir . . . but they are unable in any degree to extend them." Mr. Griffin's letter of June 14 to the Amir omits some of the qualifications given

It is of the first importance to appreciate exactly the nature and significance of these engagements. They do not appear to have been asked for by the Afghans, but to have arisen from the initiative of the British Government. Their purpose is to warn off

---

in the letter sent for his instruction, and the Amir's reply leaves out some of the qualifications that Mr. Griffin had retained. But in his reviewing despatch of December 3, 1880, Lord Hartington, with all the papers before him, wrote to approve the proceedings of the Indian Government without reference to these modifications. In 1885 the same Cabinet somewhat extended even the words of Sir L. Griffin. Sir Lepel Griffin writes in 1889 (*l. c.*) that " England is as much bound in honour to defend Herat, Maimana, Balkh, or any other portion of Afghanistan against Russia as she is to defend the Isle of Wight against France." The instructions which he was entrusted to carry out contain the most positive statements that no such obligation was contemplated by the Government which he served. The statements in the text give the exact state of the pledges so far as they are known. But the delimitation, coupled with the speeches on the vote of credit and at Rawal Pindi, must be considered at least as important as the negotiations of 1880, and as even more effectual in committing Great Britain to Afghanistan.

Russia and to secure the assistance of Afghanistan in the defence of India against Russia. The promises of 1873 were made under Mr. Gladstone's first, and those of 1880 and 1885 under his second, administration. They have not been the subject of party criticism.

The condition that the Amir should accept British direction in his foreign relations seems to have been imposed upon him. Shere Ali preferred a Russian alliance to the limited promises given him by England, and Abdurrahman in 1880 declared himself anxious to stand equally well with both Powers. He was told, however, that the two Powers were agreed that he should be under British protection, and accordingly he accepted this condition and the accompanying guarantees. He has received, and is still receiving, large subsidies which have enabled him to assert his authority in Afghan Turkestan and Herat— to his Afghan subjects foreign countries. The Afghans themselves would probably not willingly fight for the defence of these provinces, which are held by the Amir's paid troops. But they will fight almost to a man for the independence of their own hills and valleys.

The engagements then operate primarily as a notice to Russia, that a violation of the border is a *casus belli* with the British Empire. Upon this and upon British money rests the Amir's possession of Herat and Turkestan.

To forecast the conduct of the Amir and the Afghans it is not necessary to frame an uncertain hypothesis about their character. A simpler plan is to put ourselves in their place, and ask what our own feelings and conduct would be in the same circumstances. If a Russian occupation of Herat and Afghan Turkestan were permitted by Great Britain, the Amir would hold that he was released from all obligations, and that he had been betrayed. His bitterness against the English would be extreme. Supposing the event to happen after the death of Abdurrahman, the Afghans

of Kabul would have the same feeling, for the
first letter to Abdurrahman assumes a general
and continuous relation between Great Britain
and Afghanistan, in the nature of a protectorate. Upon the death, however, of the
Amir, if there should be difficulties about the
succession, the dependencies (Herat and Turkestan) will probably revolt, giving a pretext for
Russian interference ; and the Afghans will
be more concerned with the domestic trouble
than with these foreign provinces.

It is conceivable that the Amir or the
Afghans, or both, might acquiesce in a Russian
occupation of the dependencies rather than in
the march of British troops through their own
country ; and that in any case they would
prefer the protectorate of Russia to that of
England, whose heavy hand has more than
once been laid upon them.

The eventuality for which British policy
has to be prepared is that of a Russian force
crossing the delimited frontier and the Oxus,

and marching upon Herat and into Afghan Turkestan.

If the Afghans resist this invasion and appeal for English help, such help cannot be refused without arousing the just resentment of the Afghans, and spreading through India the belief that Russia is the stronger Power. But to give the help required would not be easy.

In order to eject the Russians from Afghan Turkestan, a counter-attack would have to be made, for which there is no possible route except that through Herat. An army moving northwards from Herat would threaten all the communications of a Russian force in Afghan Turkestan, and would thus paralyse all Russian movements between Khamiab and Badakshan. It would hardly affect the Russian communications from the Syr Daria to Ferghana and the Pamir, so that in that quarter any Russian attack would have to be met by direct local resistance.

A properly planned Russian invasion would have defeated the Afghan armies in Turkestan, and pushed its outposts to the watershed line, and its main body to Herat, before English troops could, at any of these points, anticipate the attackers. Herat is less than 100 miles from the present Russian outposts between the Murghab and the Hari Rud. It is 350 miles from the British outposts at the Khwaja Amran. The Russian preparations for the concentration of troops would precede the counter-preparations in India, and in this way probably a month's start would be gained. Not less than five weeks would at present be required for the concentration of two army corps at Quetta, and at least another month, on a low estimate, for the march to Herat. Herat has been strengthened under the advice of English officers, and has an Afghan garrison. But that it could resist a siege of two or three months' duration is far from certain. The probability is that the English

M

would arrive to find the place held by a
Russian garrison, and covered by a Russian
field army.

The English counter-attack would then be
heavily handicapped. It would have to begin
with the recapture of Herat, which in
European hands would be a strong fortress.
Moreover, under present conditions, the army
charged with the recapture would have to rely
for the transport of its supplies upon camels
and pack-mules working from a base 350
miles distant.

The operation would be facilitated by the
prolongation, before the commencement of
hostilities, of the railway towards Herat, a
measure to which the Amir and the Afghans
are understood to object. The objection shows
that the Afghans are more fearful of British
power than anxious for British help, and that
it is unwise to count upon them. The difficulty thus created in the way of making
preparations adequate to the promises given,

suggests the idea of modifying the promises, and reducing them to what can be made good with existing preparations. But this would probably further alienate the Afghans, and would amount to an invitation to the Russians, who would sooner or later hear of it, to annex Herat and Afghan Turkestan.

Suppose the first stage of Russian advance —to the watershed line—to have been effected. This advance might take place equally if the Afghans asked for but did not receive British aid; if they resisted the Russians while deprecating British aid; or if they acquiesced in the Russian advance. The question arises, what guarantees could the British Government then obtain against the second stage, the Russian advance to Kabul and Kandahar?

Everything depends upon the attitude of the Afghans after this first Russian move. Their acceptance of British assistance, on the understanding that their independence should be respected, would render possible a policy

M 2

quite different from that which would be
forced upon a British Government by their
hostility, or perhaps even by a doubtful
attitude on their part.   In the former event,
that of a friendly Afghanistan, the presence at
Quetta or Pishin of two army corps, or of one
army corps with a second at hand to support
it at short notice, would probably suffice.   But
these two army corps could not be removed
or used for any other purpose.   If the
Afghans were unfriendly it would be necessary to advance the British frontier to the
Helmand, and to fortify a position near
Girishk, as well as one near Ghazni.

In the northern portion of the country there
could be no assurance that the Russians, even
if opposed by the Afghans, could not anticipate
the English at Kabul.   The passes of the
Hindu Kush and Koh-i-Baba are nearer to
Kabul than the nearest English posts at Thal
and the east end of the Khaibar.   The Irak
Pass is nearer to Kabul than Kuram.   If

the British border remains where it is, the Russians at Bamian can always be the first at Kabul. Even if the British border were pushed nearer, say to the Shutargardan and Gandamak, the Russians, having the initiative, would still have the chances on their side, as they would gain the time that would be needed to warn the English outposts that they had started. To advance the British border to the Shutargardan and Gandamak would have the disadvantage but not the advantage of annexation. It would turn the Afghans into enemies, but leave them free to fight against the British. If, therefore, the Afghans were disposed to prefer the Russians to the British it would be necessary for the English, unless they were willing to acquiesce in the occupation of Kabul by the Russians, to occupy it with their own troops, that is, practically, to annex what would be left of Afghanistan by pushing forward the British border to the Helmand and the Hindu Kush.

If the British Government should acquiesce in the Russian occupation, not only of Herat and Afghan Turkestan, but also of Kabul, the defence of India would become a difficult, if not a hazardous matter. The Russians would have advanced bases at Kabul and Herat, and would protect Kabul by the fortification of the passes leading to Jalálábad. Their first object would then be to obtain Kandahar, and thus to secure the co-operation between their wings. This done they would be free to choose their line of attack. An advance eastwards from Kalat-i-Ghilzai or Ghazni would threaten at once all the passes of the Sulimans and the communications of Quetta. The English armies divided by the Sulimans would be operating in two separate theatres of war.

The defensive organisation of the British frontier would involve, first, that communication between these two theatres of war should be created by a railway through the Sulimans. The line would probably run from

Attock or Kushalgarh by Kohat and Bannu to the Gumal Pass, and thence by the Zhob valley to Quetta. In the second place, British authority would need to be established in the Suliman country up to the watershed of the Indus, and the allegiance of the Pathan tribes as far as possible secured. Thirdly, it would be desirable to hold not only Kandahar but Ghazni, in order to keep a good distance apart the two wings of the Russian attack. It will be seen that the fundamental measure is the construction of the railway through the Sulimans, which would be the most effective means both of securing the friendship of the Pathans and of approaching Ghazni.

It appears to us that this railway, which is necessary to the defence of the country at present held by Great Britain, should be constructed without delay. The Gumal is the chief trade route between India and Afghanistan. It is followed every year by thousands of native traders with their caravans, and a

railway through it would lead not only to the
establishment of better relations with tribes
whose attitude is of great importance for
defence, but also to a better knowledge of the
country within the curve of the Sulimans, at
present, to the north of the Zhob valley,
unsurveyed and practically unknown.   The
Suliman railway commits the British Government to no policy except the defence of the
present Indian frontier.

A second railway, that from Peshawar to
Kabul, would bring about a closer, perhaps a
really friendly relation with the Afghans, and
would make it not only practicable but easy
to anticipate the Russians at Kabul.

If the peace should last until the completion
of these railways, the steps which would aim
at the defence of Herat or a counter-offensive
through that place might then be considered.
They are, first, a railway from the Khwaja
Amran towards and if possible up to Herat,
and secondly, a direct railway from the coast

of Baluchistan in the direction of the same city. If this last-named line had reached the latitude of Quetta on the outbreak of hostilities, the difficulty of transport to Herat might be overcome.

The force that will be required for the defence of India depends upon that available for the attack. The Russians have an unlimited number of troops upon which to draw, and for any enterprise of a special nature can pick elements of special fitness. The force with which they can undertake any of the various operations we have contemplated is limited only by their available means of transport and supply. At the terminus of their railway they can collect any number of troops, and can easily feed by the railway four army corps. The railway will always closely follow the advance of their border.

The policy of counter-attack would therefore require at least four army corps, besides the garrisons of India and of the frontier. The

Indian armies are not an unlimited store of
troops that can be freely drawn upon for
operations on the border. At present they
could furnish two army corps for this purpose.
Perhaps by a judicious change in the recruiting of the native troops, rejecting all the
unwarlike races and enlisting only men of the
best fighting class, the force available for
active employment even against Russian
troops could be increased. But whenever the
operations come to require any much larger
force than the two army corps now available
in India, the excess will have to be drawn
from Great Britain, or from Great Britain and
the colonies. Two army corps would, then,
have to be sent from England. If the policy
of abandoning Herat to a Russian advance,
but of occupying Kabul and Kandahar in
that event, be adopted, no immediate increase
of the Indian Army would be needed. But
as soon as the Russian preparation of their
new base was completed (including the rail-

way from Sarakhs to Herat, and perhaps to Mazar-i-Sharif), a Russian force such as that named above would become available, and therefore a reinforcement of the Indian Army by two corps would equally be required.

The same condition as to reinforcement applies to the policy which would abstain from the annexation of Kabul, and wait within the present frontier for the development of the Russian attack.

If the mere defensive is adopted, whether on the Kabul-Kandahar line or on the present border, the defending forces must be kept permanently quartered near to the frontier. It would be unsafe to trust to their passage from England to Quetta in time to anticipate a Russian attack, of which the shortest possible notice would be given.

The chief objection, apart from British treaty obligations, to an advance of the Russian border is that it would diminish Russian transport difficulties for a further advance, and thus increase the force with which the defenders of India must afterwards cope.

It appears then, on a review of the subject, that the cost of Indian defence in men and fortifications, and consequently in money, will be increased by every advance of the Russian border.

The difficulties of every kind connected with an English advance to Herat or Kabul have been shown. From a merely strategic point of view, however, the occupation of Herat would effectually stop the Russian advance, and the occupation and fortification of Kabul and Kandahar by the British would also render hopeless Russian attempts at further progress. But so long as there is reasonable hope that the Afghans will themselves resist Russian invasion, and will accept British help for the purpose, it would be imprudent to push any measures not acceptable to them.

The defence of the present British frontier

would be extremely difficult and costly, and if this policy be adopted as one to be persevered in, in the event of a Russian advance, the anxiety of Indian statesmen will be grave and lasting. British preparations should take the shape of perfecting, as far as may be, the communications behind the present outposts ; of winning by every just means the confidence and loyalty of the border tribes between the Indus and the kingdom of Kabul ; and of increasing in every way the efficiency of the Indian armies. Whatever measures are taken, and whatever policy may be adopted, the fundamental condition of the defence of India will continue to be the readiness of England to send ample reinforcements when they are needed. In other words, the peace of India depends upon Great Britain having an efficient army at home and retaining the command of the sea.

CHAPTER V.

THE ARMIES.

THE difficulties of British Army administration arise mainly from the necessity to provide for three distinct and very dissimilar services— at home, in India, and in colonial garrisons.

Twenty years ago, when the old long-service recruiting had broken down, the attempt was made to adopt the Continental plan, which, by means of a short term of service with the colours and a much longer reserve liability, yields a large force upon mobilisation. But a three years' service is incompatible with the Indian and colonial duties. Recruits have in England always been taken at eighteen. No

man is fit to stand the climate of India until
he is twenty. A recruit enlisted at nineteen,
and sent to India after a year's training, could
not, if he is entitled to pass into the reserve in
two years more, be kept in India for even two
years, so that the expense of perpetual passages
to and fro would be enormous.

The same objection prevents the employment of three years' men in the colonies. To
meet it a compromise has been made. The
present system is enlistment for a twelve
years' term, of which eight, seven, or fewer
years are spent with the colours, and the remainder in the reserve. The eight years'
term is enforced in the case of men whose
battalions take them abroad. For the others
seven years is the rule, but there are many
exceptions by the frequent discharge of men
into the reserve after three or more years'
service with the colours.

The system has provided on the whole
satisfactorily, though not cheaply, for India

and the colonies. But it has ruined the home army, both from the point of view of administration and of war training.

In the method adopted the battalion is the unit. The army has altogether 141 line battalions. Each of these takes its turn for a few years at a time to serve in India or a colony. A list or *roster* of battalions is kept, in which the headings are, roughly speaking, home, low establishment; home, high establishment; India, or a colony. Each battalion keeps passing through this set of stages. Whilst abroad its numbers need constant feeding from home to cover loss by death and sickness. To render this possible, a depot or staff of a few officers and drill-sergeants, who enlist and drill recruits, is maintained at home for each battalion* abroad.

In order to make shift with a number of depots equal to half the total number of bat-

* This is the theory. In practice, one or two battalions abroad are without depots at home.

talions, the battalions were at first "linked" in pairs and afterwards joined into two-battalion regiments. The depot belongs to the regiment, and each regiment is supposed always to have one battalion at home and one abroad. But in practice the home battalion cannot be kept at its own depot.

The net result is a perpetual shifting of battalions, not only between England, India, and the colonies, but between the several stations at home. This shifting makes it impossible to form permanent units larger than the battalion, and consequently every battalion is kept in direct relation with the central administration at the War Office, the only permanent administrative institution except the battalion itself.

Here is the main flaw in the system—the chief cause of the breakdown now universally admitted. No changes at the War Office will remedy this, for as long as the army consists of 141 ever-moving battalions,

N

the War Office will be the only fixed administrative body, and decentralisation is impossible. So long as the War Office has to superintend the affairs of battalions, it cannot manage the general affairs of the army; it cannot attend to the national defence.

In order to set free the War Office to devote itself to the general management of the army, the shifting of battalions must be stopped. Each battalion of the army at home must have a home, so that its supervision can be entrusted to a local military authority. But the shifting cannot be stopped without stopping also the practice of sending troops abroad.

The cessation of the present system of perpetual motion is not less imperatively demanded in the interest of military training. An army in the field consists of a number of army corps, each of which consists of divisions, and these again of brigades, the brigade itself being a combination of a number of battalions.

Success depends upon the skill with which army corps, divisions, and brigades are handled, and this skill can only be acquired by constant practice. Even the handling of the battalion has two distinct aspects. It is one thing to command a battalion by itself, but quite another thing, and a much more difficult one, to handle it as a portion of a brigade, so as to ensure its co-operation towards the fulfilment of the purpose of the brigadier.

In the British Army no unit higher than the battalion has a permanent existence, though at Aldershot a few brigades, of which the elements are constantly changing, are maintained. It follows that in the British Army the art of handling the army corps, and the division as part of an army corps, is absolutely unknown. There may be officers who have studied its theory in Continental treatises ; there is not one who has in this department the facility resulting from practice which is denoted by the term skill. The art of commanding the divi-

N 2

sion by itself, and the brigade as a part of the
division, is acquired to a limited extent by the
very few generals who are fortunate enough to
be appointed to commands at Aldershot, or in
India. As a rule, the British officer has no
opportunity of perfecting himself in any of
that portion of the art of command which goes
beyond the sphere of the isolated battalion, and
which is the special function of the general
officer.

The British Army at home, in short, has
no generals, and can have none until its battalions are settled and grouped into brigades,
divisions, and army corps. In the absence of
generals, there is no guarantee that even the
elementary work, the training and handling of
battalions, is conducted on principles calculated
to insure their fitness as component parts of
an army.

It is therefore indispensable, in the interest
of the home army, and in order to make its
administration and training possible, that it

should be freed from the necessity of maintaining by its reliefs the British Army in India,
and the garrisons of the naval stations. The
possibility of freeing the home army from this
incubus depends, of course, upon the conditions
of the Indian and colonial services. If they
can be provided for without maintaining a
system that ruins the home service the change
becomes imperative. An examination will
show that it is not open to objection from the
point of view of the interest of Indian and
colonial defence.

The Indian Government defrays the entire
cost of the Indian armies, whether incurred in
India or at home, and administers them on its
own authority, with the exception of three
branches. The recruiting of the British forces
in India, the appointments to many of the
responsible offices, and the supply of a portion
of the munitions of war, are conducted by the
British War Office. The Indian Government
maintains and manages two armies, a British

one of 73,000, and a native one of 145,000 men. These considerable forces (218,000 men) cost India altogether Rx. 20,677,814, of which nearly three quarters are spent in India, and more than one quarter (Rx. 5,733,719 or £3,957,703) is spent in Great Britain.*

* Rough abstract of actual cost of Indian Army (year ended March 31, 1890).

I. In India.

	Rx.
Command, administration, and regimental cost of whole British and native forces	7,900,000
Auxiliary services and charges . .	6,090,000
Pensions	900,000
Sea transport paid for in India . .	50,000
Total	Rx. 14,940,000

II. In England.

	£
Pensions	2,050,000
Miscellaneous charges for auxiliary services, *e.g.*, ordnance and clothing . . .	530,000
Officers on furlough, and pay of regiments on voyage out and home . . .	304,600
Sea transport charges	222,500
Payment to Imperial Government . .	849,500
Total	£3,956,600

The payment of this sum by India to England is remarkable, for the amount is the largest item in the whole of the Indian accounts. It exceeds the total cost of the British force in India, together with the expense of its command and administration. It far exceeds the total cost of the native force. Much of it is, however, indispensable. Pensions alone, which are a necessary part of any system for employing Europeans in India, account for more than two millions sterling. A quarter of a million is paid for ordnance stores. An almost equal amount is absorbed by the cost of transporting the reliefs or annual contingents of time-expired men and their successors from and to India.

There is, however, one item which cannot be thus admitted as inevitable. The Indian accounts show under the heading "Regimental pay, allowances and charge for the European army," a sum of £849,588 paid to the Imperial Government. Of this amount

£197,000 were arrears from previous years. The remainder is the "sum to be received in aid of army estimates to meet the home effective charges for the regular forces serving in India," which, in the British Army Estimates, figures at £700,000 in 1890–1, and at £750,000 in 1891–2.

This is the price that India pays for its British recruits, in addition to the cost of their sea-voyage out and home, and of their pay while on passage. It is a monstrous price to pay. It exceeds the whole cost of the general staff and administration of the two Indian armies; it equals the amount charged in the English Estimates for the Volunteer force or for the Militia service. It amounts to about £75 for each English soldier received by India, that is, it is more than three years' pay for each man.

The average annual cost of a British soldier, not being a commissioned officer, is about £55 a year. For £750,000 a year, therefore, the

Indian Government could afford every year to enlist 10,000 men in England; to keep them in barracks, well officered, for a year, to find them manœuvring grounds, and give them a first-rate military training.

The £750,000 is not paid for any direct service, or for the maintenance of a single recruit. All the charges incurred by India in England are met out of the rest of the £4,000,000.

The £750,000 is simply a tribute paid by India to the War Office for the privilege of receiving British regiments on loan at India's expense from the moment they leave England until the day when they are safely landed back again. If the tribute were remitted, the Indian Government could afford for a fraction of it to keep recruiting offices in the United Kingdom and in Canada, which would be able to supply all the men required, and with the balance to pension every one of its time-expired soldiers at the rate of a shilling a day for life.

The annual supply of men is the sole advantage accruing to the Indian Government from the connection between its army and the home army. The appointments could be as well made by the Indian Government as by the War Office; and the Indian Army, if free to buy its stores where it chose, would buy from the War Office just so long as the War Office offered the best value for the money.

India, therefore, by the freedom to provide its supply of British soldiers in its own way, would gain to the amount of £750,000 a year, no small matter to an administration whose revenues have little capacity of expansion.

All the colonial stations at which British troops are now kept are—directly or indirectly —naval bases.* They are really garrisoned for the benefit of the fleet. The garrisons must be long-service troops, and require a

* Natal forms, perhaps, an exception to this rule.

training different from that needed by the home army. They must be either garrison gunners, or infantry skilled in the defence of works. The corps of Royal Marines is the ideal body of troops for the purpose. This force at present is 14,000 strong, and costs about a million a year. The colonial garrisons absorb about double that number of troops, and cost about two millions a year. The existing 14,000 marines have already duties to perform. But there would be no difficulty in transferring two millions from the Army to the Navy Estimates, and empowering the Admiralty to raise extra marines sufficient to garrison the various naval bases. The very great advantage would then be secured of having the naval bases, the ships for which they exist, and which have to protect them, and the garrisons of their forts, under the undivided command and administration of a single authority—the Admiralty.

Our proposal, therefore, is that the three

services now administered from the War Office should be severed; the naval stations handed over to the Admiralty; the Indian Government entrusted with the entire control of the Indian military system; and the War Office charged solely with its share in the general management of Imperial defence, and with the raising, maintenance and training of the home forces.

The present distribution of the army, which numbers roughly about 200,000 men, is that half are in the United Kingdom and the other half in the Colonies and India, the British force in India being slightly over 70,000 men. We propose to accept these figures as a working basis. The Indian Army is sufficient for the peace requirements of India. A force of 100,000 men at home, with a reserve of 60,000, is just sufficient to supply in case of war the two army corps which would be needed for India, and the two which should form the first portion of the field army at home. In case the garrisons of fortresses at home were composed of regulars, there would not be sufficient troops left to form one army corps besides the two destined for the help of India. The present numbers may be taken as an irreducible minimum, especially when we remember that India has virtually no reserves of her own from which to fill up the gaps of war.

Postponing for later examination the Militia and Volunteers, we may now give the outline of the plan which seems suitable for the needs of the regular forces at home. Recruits would be enlisted at eighteen for ten years, of which only three would be spent with the colours, the remaining seven in the reserve. The abolition of stoppages would secure to the men a full shilling a day. There are good grounds for supposing that this reduction of the term spent with the colours would facilitate recruiting. A lad of eighteen has no great value in the labour market, and when discharged at twenty-one will have no more difficulty in finding employment than if he had never seen the army at all. The present discharged soldier of twenty-five or twenty-six is in a much more difficult position, and the frequent calls which have been made on the reserve have rendered his chances of employment precarious.

The reserve ought never to be called upon for actual service, except in the event of a war requiring the whole military resources of the nation. If this condition were assured, the reserve man would be unprejudiced in the labour market, and the chief hindrance in the way of recruiting would disappear. It is doubtful whether pay should be given to reserve men, except for trainings, manœuvres, or actual service ; but an Act of Parliament should make it impossible to call out the reserve for actual warfare, except in the event of war with a first-rate Power.

If this were the system at home the Indian Government would be able to arrange its own service on the basis of an enlistment for a long term of service followed by pension or money gift. No transfer should be allowed from the home to the Indian service during the three years' term. But every man on the conclusion of his third year should be offered the Indian engagement, provided the necessary Indian contingent were not exceeded. The man so engaging for India would then be discharged from the home service, which would have no more claim upon him.

The first result of this system will be to give a very much larger force available for war, without increasing the actual peace establishment; or to enable the force at present available for war to be obtained from a much-reduced peace establishment. At the same time the Indian Army will be maintained at its present strength, with only picked long-service soldiers, and without any additional

cost over the charges now incurred.* We
assume that the present peace establishment
(say 105,000 men at home) will be maintained.
The home army, after the system has come
into full operation, will be able to put in the
field seven and a half army corps, so that
there will be no difficulty in despatching aid
to India and the garrisons. But if even the
peace establishment were reduced by more

---

* The effects of the change proposed may be seen
in the following figures, which are given by way of
illustration, and in the calculation of which it has
been assumed that an annual contingent of any given
number of men loses 5 per cent. of its numbers in each
successive year. This is, we believe, a liberal allow-
ance for waste, even in India, where it will, after the
eighth year of service, be higher than at home.

The calculation is based on the assumption of an
eighteen years' term in India. We have, however,
satisfied ourselves that a twelve years', or even an eight
years' term (these being, apparently, the periods most
favourably regarded by Indian officials), would be
practicable, without entailing for pension, or other
arrangement upon discharge, any noteworthy additional
burden upon Indian Finance. In making the calculation, it is necessary to assume a rigid and uniform
term, but in practice it would be better to make the

than a quarter (a saving of over two millions a year), the home army would still turn out for war 165,000 men (four and a half army corps), the force at present available if the reserve be called out.

---

term as elastic as possible—that is, to make it easy for a soldier tired of his trade to leave it at any time.

I. If (as we assume) the numbers of the force at present kept in the United Kingdom be retained (105,000), then under the proposed system the annual contingent of troops will be 36,809

Diminishing in its second year of service to . 34,969

And in its third year to 33,221

The total force at any time with the colours in Great Britain will be 104,999

When a contingent enters upon its fourth year, 6,000 of its men will enlist in the Indian Service, and the remainder, 27,221, will pass into the reserve at home. Eighteen contingents of 6,000 men will yield 72,000 men, the strength of the British Army in India, while seven contingents of 27,221 (starting less 5 per cent., i.e., at 25,860) will yield 156,021 men, the home reserve. The home force available on mobilisation will be 105,000 + 156,000, i.e., say, 260,000 men, about seven and a half army corps.

The numerical or financial benefit is, however, the smallest. The real advantage of the plan is, for the home army, that it will make it possible to give every battalion, battery, and squadron a permanent home, and so to form permanent brigades, divisions, and army corps.

II. If the basis taken were the present yield of men of the home army (165,000), the figures would be :

	For Home.	For India
Annual contingent . .	25,048 = 18,083 +	6,965
Second year . . .	23,796	
Third year . . .	22,608	
Total with colours at home	71,452	

In the fourth year there would go—

To RESERVE—	To INDIAN ARMY—
15,505, of whom seven contingents will yield 93,546 (reserve).	5,972, of whom eighteen contingents will yield 72,000 men, the present force of the Indian Army.
Total available . 71,452	
93,546	
————	
164,998	

the present yield for war.

The administration can then be decentralised, and the War Office relieved of detail. The army can be properly trained, because it will have army corps commanders, that is, skilled generals—it will at least be the fault of the War Office if its generals do not become skilful, for they will have the opportunity—and lastly, the fact that the bodies of troops will each have its home, will render mobilisation as simple, swift, and sure as it is in any country in the world.

Next we come to the cost for pension for 21 years to every discharged soldier of the Indian Army (after 18 years' Indian service). When the system is in full work there will be 21 contingents, of which each at the outset will represent the 19th contingent of an original 6,000 men. A contingent of 6,000 becomes in the 19th year 2,382. The sum of a yearly contingent of 2,382 after 21 years (with a waste in each contingent of 5 per cent. per annum) is 31,417. A pension of 1s. a day for 31,417 men amounts to £573,360 per annum. Accordingly, the sum now paid to England by India would cover the extra cost of pensions to all men after 18 years' Indian service, and leave a margin of £176,000.

The great advantage to the Indian Army,
besides those which have been already explained, will be to free its administration from
some of the fetters at present imposed upon
it.   All Indian administrators, civil as well
as military, have for many years wished to
put an end to the divided command, which
survives from the old-fashioned Presidency
system.   The existence in Bombay and Madras
of commanders-in-chief, and consequent absence of unity of command in India, is perhaps
the weakest point of the existing Indian
military system.

The proposals here made are by no means
revolutionary.   They involve merely that the
battalions, squadrons, and batteries in India
should remain there, that those at home
should remain at home, and that the conditions of enlistment should be modified in
the manner described.   A number of battalions and batteries might be transferred to
the Admiralty, to form with the marines the

colonial force. The officers of all ranks should be interchangeable between the three services, and all reasonable facilities for exchange afforded.

It would perhaps be wise to strengthen the infantry element of the British force in India, and to assign to the home army a larger share of the cavalry than at present. The home army has a large force of infantry in the Militia and the Volunteers, and should be proportionately stronger in cavalry and field artillery.

It has been suggested that, if our view of the nature of naval defence were adopted, the Volunteers and the Militia, so far as their home use is concerned, would be unnecessary. This might become true if the Navy were raised to the strength which we have recommended, and there were no uncertainty as to the nature of future operations at sea. As matters stand, it is undoubtedly necessary to make the most of the provision against possible invasion represented by the Militia and Volunteers.

The Volunteers, and the Militia as soon as the short-service system at home is so far in working order as to relieve the Militia of the function of obtaining and preparing recruits for the line, should be organised with a view to their use in war. Those regiments which are destined to garrison fortresses, or commercial ports at home, should be grouped into garrison or local defence bodies, and receive a constitution and training suitable for this, their war work. The remaining Volunteer and Militia troops should be formed into Volunteer and Militia army corps, comprising all the necessary arms, and every necessary auxiliary service, such as transport and commissariat. Each army corps, as well as each division and brigade, should have a permanent commander, a fully-paid officer, selected as the fit war leader and peace instructor of his command.

The expense of this arrangement would be very slight. It would render possible the more thorough instruction of the Militia and Volunteer officers, their proper supervision, and the selection of the most capable for promotion. For all the commands in their own branch up to that of the army corps, Militia and Volunteer officers should be eligible, without their having any special right or claim to preference. This would give the opportunity for the advancement of such of them as show real military capacity, and would be a valuable incentive to activity for the whole body.

With regard to the Volunteers, the greatest obstacle to their improvement has hitherto been the difficulty which the head-quarters staff has found in appreciating the real conditions and needs of the force. This would be removed by the selection of Volunteer officers as members of the Volunteer department in the staff of the War Office. The promises made to the Volunteers for the provision of ranges, and for the payment of necessarily incurred debts, must of course be fulfilled.

CHAPTER VI.

THE MANAGEMENT OF THE HOME ARMY.

ANY system proposed for the better management of the army must satisfy three distinct conditions. It must be framed with a view to the preparation of the army for war; it must secure unimpaired the authority of the Cabinet; and it must provide for an efficient control over expenditure by the House of Commons.

The fundamental requirement is, of course, that the necessities of war shall be aimed at, and that the system shall involve a minimum of change in the passage from peace to war. The steps necessarily taken when a war becomes imminent are well known. The Cabinet chooses the general thought fittest to have

the conduct of the operations, and calls upon
him for a scheme or " plan of campaign." If
this is approved of, the general is given the
command, is entrusted with the execution of
his plan, and is given full authority and support within the limits of the enterprise. The
general thus appointed is alone responsible,
and his responsibility to the Cabinet is direct.

It is a recognised principle that the same
general plans and executes. One officer is not
asked to be responsible for carrying out as
commander the plan made by another. This
was illustrated in the preparations for the
Nile campaign. General Stephenson did not
approve of the Nile route, which Lord
Wolseley thought a good one. Accordingly,
Lord Wolseley was appointed to the command,
and not General Stephenson, who had at first
been consulted.

The next proceeding is to make ready or
" mobilise " the various bodies of troops to be
employed, and to collect them at the place or

places which the general has suggested as most suitable. The operations of the campaign then begin, the general conducting the movements upon his own authority.

Substituting in some countries king or emperor or viceroy for Cabinet, this is the method of all armies. It was that of Prussia in 1866 and in 1870 ; it is that followed in India whenever there is a military expedition.

In Great Britain in our own time the practice has been when war begins to pass over the commander-in-chief. This office is thus unreal. In all probability successive Cabinets have shrunk from the risk of constitutional danger or trouble that would be incurred if a near relative of the king, acting with the authority necessary for a commander in war, should be employed to command in chief in the field.

The first requirement of a sound system is a general who can be entrusted with the duty of advising the Cabinet upon the conduct of wars, and with the actual management of campaigns. To have such an officer is indispensable, for it is an elementary truth that war can never be well conducted by a committee.

The second stage of war is the actual conduct of the operations. For this purpose an army in the field is built up of parts, each complete in itself, called army corps. The army also has a distinct group of forces, forming a separate sub-command, upon its line of communications. The work of the war-commander consists in sending to the generals of army corps and to the general of communications written orders in which he explains so much of his purpose as is needful for them to know, and tells them in what way the bodies they command are to co-operate for its attainment. He watches over the fulfilment of his orders, and has power to exact obedience. The general of communications takes the commander's orders for provisions (so far as they are not to be had on the spot where the army is), for men and horses to replace losses, and for weapons and tools. These supplies he receives from those officials at home whose business it is to provide them, and forwards to the army, where they are distributed according to the commander's instructions.

The object of military organisation is to create and get into working order in peace this machinery for war, which embraces :—

(1.) The commander and his office or " staff."

(2.) A number of army corps.

(3.) A line of communications.

(4.) Arrangements for supplying the line of communications from home.

Each of these four heads needs a brief explanation to show that it is indispensable, and that no scheme that omits it will meet the requirements of war.

(1.) The commander is the architect of the

campaign, though his art differs from an architect's, in that the design must adapt itself from day to day to the enemy's movements, an unknown quantity to be discovered.

A commander always requires some assistance. His orders must be written and copied'; his correspondence with his generals of corps and communications must be prompt ; he must keep stock of all information about the enemy and the country, and all that is done must be precisely recorded. Accordingly, the commander needs a number of secretaries, who, to be useful, must be trained to his methods and familiar with the nature of his duties. This body of secretaries is his general staff.

The head secretary authorised to sign in the commander's name, and to represent him, as far as may be in his temporary absences from the office, is called in foreign armies " Chief of the staff." This was the position nominally held by Moltke, but his paper on councils of war shows that the title was inappropriate, and that he was really the commander of the army in the sense in which we have described that office. The king represented the government of the nation, which must always retain the supreme authority. There can be no object in copying in England the names of German posts which correspond to nothing in the English system.

The essential features of the German system, so far as our present subject is concerned, were, during the life of Moltke, first, that the commander for war is chosen beforehand, and given authority to prepare himself and his assistants for their war functions; secondly, that the organisation of the army in peace into army corps does away with the need for a great central office like the British War Office; and thirdly, that as the commander (called chief of the staff) has not in peace to manage battalions, he is free to study the art of command, and to practise

it in the autumn manœuvres. His office or
set of secretaries thus learn during peace how
to write orders for an army, the peculiar
business of a commander-in-chief.

These three things are essential in any
army. They have been adopted all over the
Continent since 1870 ; and the American Civil
War shows how, before the Prussian successes,
a nation unready for war learned, during four
years' bitter experience, to find a commander,
and to give him full authority ; how the
army-corps system developed itself ; and how
successive commanders suffered until a staff
able to write orders had grown up.

In our judgment, then, any reform of the
army must begin with the selection by the
Cabinet of a general whom they trust. His
duties will be to advise the Cabinet upon
the conduct of possible wars, on the understanding that he will be called upon to
execute his plans if they are accepted, and
that if they are not approved of, he will be

relieved of his post and otherwise honourably employed. He must be given full authority over the army, subject to the limitations hereafter explained, and will in particular select his own staff. It matters little what this officer is called. It would be most natural to make him commander-in-chief. There would be no harm in calling him chief of the staff. But it is essential that he have authority, limited only by that of the Cabinet, to carry out, during peace, the preparation of the army for war.

The proposal made by Lord Hartington's commission to form a "department of the Chief of the Staff," with no authority over the army, but with general power to meddle, rests upon a misrepresentation of the working at any rate of the German Army. Imitation we hold to be always a mistake. In this case the imitation consists only in borrowing a name, while ignoring the nature and real merits of the system set up to be copied.

P

Count Moltke, in 1890, writing with special reference to the question of reform in the British Army, and to the proposal for the formation of a general staff, said : " A general staff cannot be improvised on the outbreak of war. It must have been prepared long before, during peace, and must be in practical working and in constant touch with the troops. But that is not enough. The general staff must know who its future commander will be, must be in close touch with him and acquire his confidence, without which its position is untenable.

" The advantage is great when the head of the state is at the same time the leader in war. . . . But the constitution does not in every country admit of placing the chief of the state at the head of the army. If the government will—and *can*—choose beforehand the most capable general for the post, he must be given in peace full authority to prepare the troops and their leaders, and to come to an understanding with his general staff. This commander will seldom be the minister of war, who during the whole war is indispensable at home, where all the threads of administration are gathered together."

Thus according to Moltke's view, which coincides with the practice of all modern armies, including that of Napoleon, an army requires a single military chief, responsible for the conception and the execution of operations. This chief requires a group of assistants, who are merely an enlargement of himself, not a separate and independent body, but the organ of the commander for communication with his subordinates, and the auxiliary or instrument of his studies. A staff without a commander is an absurdity.

Besides the commander, however, there must be a minister of war, a term which in German means the head of the department for supplying the army from home during

war. This office does not in any way correspond with that of the secretary of state for
war ; it is a military office, dealing in war
with the supply of men, horses, provisions,
weapons and stores to a mobilised army, and
in peace preparing for the exercise of these
functions.

All these posts exist in an imperfectly
defined state in the British Army. The commander-in-chief is there, but the post should
be made a real one, and its responsibility
brought home. The quartermaster-general
has many of the functions of a chief of the
staff, together with some others. If he were
relieved of the others, and the Intelligence
Department amalgamated with his office, the
requisite organ for the command would be
there, and the title quartermaster-general
need not be changed. It was that borne by
Scharnhorst, and by Count Waldersee during
the period when he was Moltke's substitute.
The minister of war described by Moltke cor-

responds closely with the old office of master-general of the ordnance, a military officer at the head of the business of supply.

(2.) The army corps is a complete sub-division of an army, and is managed entirely by the general who commands it, taking his instructions as to the purpose and nature of his movements from the commander in-chief. It consists of a number of bodies each having its own chief, so that the army corps general deals directly only with these chiefs. These bodies are two or three infantry divisions, and the groups, belonging to the army corps, of artillery, engineers, transport, commissariat, medical service, police, and post-office. Each of these bodies has a special function requiring knowledge and practice for its performance. None of them can be improvised.

If therefore an army corps when wanted for war is without any one of its necessary elements, though the rest are perfect, the corps cannot be used. If, for example, either infantry, artillery, or medical service were imperfect, the fighting power of the army corps would be impaired.   If transport or commissariat were wanting, insufficient or unskilled, its fighting power would be absolutely destroyed, for the whole force would be helpless unless men and horses were regularly fed and the troops supplied with ammunition.   The commissariat collects the food ; the transport conveys it and all other requisites to the troops.   Without these services the troops cannot enter on a campaign. Transport and commissariat duties are as difficult as those of infantry, cavalry, or artillery, and equally require special training. These branches, like the others, must therefore be trained and organised in peace. Officers and non-commissioned officers and implements must be there, with a nucleus of men and horses, to be completed to war strength on mobilisation by the recall from the reserve of men previously trained, and by the acquisition of horses previously assigned for the service.

The country should be divided into army corps districts. In each district, the whole of the infantry, cavalry, and artillery regiments, and of the transport, commissariat, and other services required for the army corps, should be permanently kept, with all the guns, powder, and shot, and other necessaries required during the opening stage of a campaign. The reserve men of each district would belong to the district army corps, every man to the regiment in which he was trained, and each man should know exactly where to go upon the publication of the order to mobilise the army. Each regiment would keep a list of its reserve men, a stock of clothing and equipment for them, and a list of horses which it would be empowered to take (upon payment, or otherwise, as settled by law) at the time of mobilisation.

The army corps in war is a moving body,

a part of the field army. All the troops of the army cannot be told off to army corps, for some are required as defenders of fortresses and commercial ports. All the troops so needed should be permanently told off to their posts, and each place to be defended should have its commandant. The defensive troops of the place should form a permanent body, organised like an army corps though otherwise composed, and under the commandant's authority.

(3.) The lines of communication in home defence would be the railways between the army and the great stores and centres of industry. The officer to be in charge of them during war ought to be appointed in peace, and provided with the necessary officers and men. His peace duty would be to prepare, under the orders of the commander-in-chief, his arrangements for all the eventualities of war that would concern him. His war business would be that of a carrier on a large scale—to receive and deliver, not to produce.

(4.) The arrangements for producing or providing the necessaries of war must also be prepared during peace. The field army corps and the local defence corps would in peace provide for most of their own wants. The supply in peace of weapons, ammunition and maps, and in war also of provisions not found in the actual theatre of war, must be carried on by other than the corps agencies.

The supply of provisions in war is the affair of the commissary general, or director of supplies, who should be appointed during peace, and with his assistants prepare his arrangements for war in accordance with the requirements explained to him by the commander-in-chief.

The supply of maps is so closely connected with the conduct of military operations, that it should be entrusted to the operations de partment of the commander-in-chief's office, already described as the general staff, or quartermaster-general's branch. Map construction in all its stages has owed most of its progress to strategy, and is therefore properly a military function.

It is otherwise with the production of weapons, in which almost every important improvement has been due to civil industry. The professional soldier is a competent judge of the merits of various weapons. He has no qualification enabling him to compete with the mechanic in their design or manufacture. In the supply of weapons, therefore, two functions should be distinguished : the choice of the weapon to be adopted, which should be left to the army ; and design and manufacture, with which the army should have nothing to do.

The selection of weapons, that is, of the patterns to be adopted, should be based upon the report of a committee formed of active combatant officers, of whom one third should

be corps or division commanders, one third
field officers, and one third captains of the arm
destined to use the weapons. The committees
should be permanent, but no member should
serve on any of them longer than two or three
years. Their sole function would be to report
upon the performance of the weapons sub-
mitted to them. They should be forbidden
to interfere with design or pattern, but empowered to make any trials whatever, and to
witness any trials offered by inventors or
manufacturers; and to report whenever in
their discretion it seemed desirable. Guarantees should be taken to exclude from these
committees all officers interested either pecu-
niarily or by connection with design or manufacture. In the choice of guns, rifles and
ammunition, the necessities of the Indian and
Colonial, as well as of the home forces, must
be taken into account, in order to secure, as
far as possible, uniformity of pattern.

Upon the decision to adopt a weapon of any

kind, it would become the duty of an officer, distinct from the selecting authority, to buy the requisite number, to distribute them to the field army and garrison corps, and to store a reserve under his own charge. He would be assisted by inspectors to guarantee the accordance of the weapons bought with the quality and design of the patterns.

The purchasing and storing officer and his agents would buy upon business principles from private firms or from Government factories. The maintenance of Government factories is desirable in those branches, such as the making of heavy guns, for which private firms are not easily induced to lay down the requisite plant. But these factories should be no part of the army, and no army officers should be employed in them.

The Government clothing department should also be removed from the army. It is no more a soldier's business to make clothes than to make guns. The principle of selection of patterns, followed by purchase in the market, applies in the one case as in the other; but the purchase of clothes should be conducted regimentally, except for certain articles, which, like weapons, must be uniform in make throughout the army.

All the branches of supply that have been discussed, except that of maps, should be managed under the authority of a single head, who might be called master-general of the ordnance, or, as Sir George Chesney proposes, master-general, and who would be an officer chosen for administrative skill. His principal subordinates would be the heads of the services of provisions, small arms and ammunition, guns and ammunition, carriages, tools, and clothing. The departments for arms and ammunition, carriages and tools would each have two branches, one for the selection of patterns, in which the head would be advised by a committee; the other for purchase and storing. The inspection might with advantage be the function of the selecting branch.

Thus the management of the army, arranged in peace with a view to war, would fall into two great branches, command and supply, directed the one by a commander-in-chief, the other by a master-general. To the commander-in-chief are assigned all that belongs to the army in the field during a campaign, that is, the staff or organ of command, a number of army corps, and the transport by which supplies are brought to the army. To the master-general are given all the services by which the supplies are prepared and handed to the transport.

Every one of the officers described must have his authority strictly defined, and will act according to principles formally laid down for his guidance. The distribution of authority is given by the organisation. Each battalion of infantry, regiment of cavalry, or group of batteries will be managed by its own commanding officer, with whom, so long as he obeys the rules, no one will be allowed to interfere, the function of his direct superior being by repeated inspection to keep him to the rules laid down.

The same arrangement will extend to the whole service, the few cases in which an appeal from the immediate authority to a higher one may be necessary being also regulated and defined. The inspecting officer will usually be the immediate superior of the one whose work is to be inspected. The sphere of action of each officer being defined by his command, it will be his duty to decide all matters that arise in that sphere, without meddling in those below it. The brigade-commander will not meddle with the internal affairs of the regiment, nor the regimental commander in those of the company ; in each case he will inspect to see that the rules have been complied with. If they have, he cannot find fault, however much he may dislike the decisions taken by his subordinate.

It is evident, then, that the rules to be formulated are of great importance. These rules are embodied in the various codes of regulations for the army and in the drill-books. One of the most important functions of the central management is to compile and modify whenever it becomes necessary these codes and drill-books. They are the law of the army, and a well-disciplined army is one in which the codes and drill-books, being rational, are fully complied with.

Their preparation and modification is at present the duty of the adjutant-general, who, however, does not act in his own name, but in that of the commander-in-chief, while some of the codes, those relating to promotion and finance, are issued in the name of the secretary of state, and sometimes in that of the Queen. The monthly army orders issued from the adjutant-general's office are modifications of these various codes. This system is probably sound. It might be better to empower the adjutant-general to sign in his own name those which he now signs "by order" of the commander-in-chief, giving the commander-in-chief a veto upon changes. No regulation ought to be issued which the commander for war does not accept. But as the adjutant-general would not sign what he himself disapproved of, a disagreement would lead to his retirement. This would make it necessary, and it is very necessary, that the adjutant-general should be in close agreement with the commander-in-chief, and would prevent the latter making use of his veto for a mere trifle.

For drill-books it would be desirable always to have committees similar in composition to those already proposed for the choice of weapons. The regulations for mobilisation should be based upon the work of a committee, and framed in concert with the quartermaster-general.　The officer who prepares and revises the codes is the proper authority to watch over their observance, and for this reason the adjutant-general becomes the organ of the commander-in-chief for the enforcement of discipline.

It remains only to examine the guarantees that are necessary to secure the authority of the Cabinet, and the financial control of the House of Commons.

The Cabinet is represented in its relations with the army by the secretary of state for war, who is also the exponent to the House of Commons of its military policy.　But by the modern practice of the constitution, the secretary of state apart from the Cabinet has no responsibility and no authority.　The Cabinet is a unit.　Every important piece of departmental policy commits the entire Cabinet, and its members stand or fall together. If the secretary of state wishes for a decision which his colleagues cannot accept, he resigns.

If they accept the decision and he remains, they share the responsibility for it. All minor matters under a sound system will be decided long before they reach the secretary of state or the Cabinet.

The Cabinet's decisions will concern only broad issues : the nature of the possible conflicts for which military preparation is required ; the occasion for the order to mobilise the forces, or for the despatch of an expedition; the modifications that may be called for in army organisation by changes in the state of the nation. One of the chief duties of the Cabinet is to select the war-commander ; that is, according to the views here set forth, the peace commander-in-chief. Another is to hold the balance between the demands of the commander-in-chief and master-general of the ordnance on the one side, and the refusals of the Treasury on the other.

The financial management of the army probably requires to be modified. The funda-

mental principle that the House of Commons
is to have supreme control of the expenditure
is sacred, and must be held sacred. But this
power of the House of Commons is at present
a mere farce, while under the pretext which
it offers, the management of the army is at
every point subject to the veto of the subordinate officials of the Treasury.

The House of Commons should require a
full and intelligible account of all military expenditure. Every one of the military chiefs
should prepare an estimate for his department.
From these estimates the financial assistant
of the secretary of state would prepare the
army estimates, in which would be embodied
the charges or savings expected from any
changes thought desirable. These estimates
would then be discussed between the chan-
cellor of the exchequer and the secretary of
state for war, the Cabinet ultimately deciding
on the total amount to be asked from the
House of Commons.

The Treasury ought to have no power to interfere with these estimates, except to object to the total sum. For if the Treasury can once object to an item, it has secured the control of the army, and the secretary of state for war and the commander-in-chief cease to have either authority or responsibility.

We have made no attempt to lay down the lines of the reforms which may be needed in the constitution of the Board of Admiralty; but we think that many of the fundamental principles which we have explained in connection with the Army are, generally speaking, applicable to the Navy also.

We attach the highest importance to the common action of the military and of the naval authorities in the consideration of Imperial defence. Any satisfactory Admiralty system will provide a competent naval adviser for the Cabinet. We doubt, however, whether it will be possible to secure unity of design in defence so long as the War Office and the

Admiralty are separately represented in the Cabinet. The difficulty would be overcome if it became the practice for one minister to hold both offices, the financial secretary of the War Office and the secretary of the Admiralty continuing to perform their present parliamentary and other duties as his subordinates.

At the conclusion of our brief enquiry we do not think it necessary to recapitulate our proposals for reform. We have not made suggestions rashly, and the changes we propose are few and simple. But we attach less weight to the details of a system than to the spirit in which it is conceived and worked. A variety of symptoms seem to us to indicate, in the military administrators of Great Britain and in the public which has tolerated their failures, a frame of mind in relation to defence which it is before all things necessary to alter.

The arrangements for the management of

the army and navy seem to have taken shape
without reference to war, for which alone the
army and navy are maintained, or to the
particular wars in which Great Britain might
possibly become involved. It is as though
the nation in its calculations had forgotten
the possibility of war.

We observe in discussions about the army
and navy the frequent use of the term " responsibility." To us the word has a distinct
meaning. It implies a connection between a
man and his acts, so that the acts are his,
and he must answer for them. But from the
lowest to the highest stages of the existing
military system we seek in vain for such a
connection. Suppose that a blunder has been
made, such, for example, as the expenditure of
large sums upon a field gun which shoots
worse than the weapon it has replaced, or upon
a rifle that proves unserviceable, or the failure
of a campaign because the plan was bad. The
present system lets no one know whose was

the act to which the breakdown was due, and who should be prevented from the repetition of such acts.

The correlative of responsibility is authority or initiative. According to our view, each officer should, in his sphere, be given full initiative. His acts, in the execution of the duties entrusted to him, should be his own, and he should bear the consequences. In other words, authority and responsibility should be realities. This is a matter of the first moment, for it is by the exercise of authority under the weight of responsibility, that character is formed, and the usefulness of an army depends largely upon the force of character of those who are at its head.

The improvement of the national defences must be a slow process ; one prolonged over many years. Acts of Parliament can modify the forms of an organisation and the machinery of its administration. But in a great institution like the army or the navy there are traditions of thought and of practice which are not easily changed. In the most favourable case, where a man of unusual insight and strength frames the reforms, he can hardly accomplish his purpose till he has trained up a new generation of subordinates. Great men, however, do not drop from heaven. They are produced by fit conditions of national life, and are representative of the national spirit, from which they derive inspiration and support. A great soldier, able to shape the defences of the British Empire in accordance at once with its military needs and with the characteristic freedom of its institutions, must be sustained by the national consciousness, recognising in him the exponent of the duty most urgent at the time.

We believe that the near future will test the British Empire, and determine whether it has a work to do in the world, and whether it has strength to do it. These questions are put to nations as to men, in the form of struggle

R

and conflict. We think that it is prudent to be prepared for such trials, and that a nation is the better for knowing its own mind as to its purposes, and as to the sacrifices it will make for their attainment. To us it seems that the tasks of civilisation and government which are suggested by the words Greater Britain are as useful to mankind as any of which history records the fulfilment, and that interference with the effort to accomplish them must therefore be resisted. At present a challenge would find the Empire half armed, and the issue would be doubtful. Our purpose in writing this book has been to urge our countrymen to prepare, while there is time, for a defence that is required alike by interest, honour, and duty, and by the best traditions of the nation's history.

LONDON : PRINTED BY WILLIAM CLOWES AND SONS, LIMITED.
STAMFORD STREET AND CHARING CROSS.